AESTHETICS: DIMENSIONS FOR MUSIC EDUCATION

Abraham A. Schwadron

MUSIC EDUCATORS NATIONAL CONFERENCE
A Department of the National Education Association
1201 Sixteenth Street NW   Washington, D. C. 20036

CONTENTS

PREFACE

It has become apparent that critical problems confronting music educators today will not be solved by reiterating well-meaning, but vague, references to desirable skills, curricula, and budgets. While these matters are important, it is paramount to provide a firm philosophical framework for contemporary music education through more penetrating and fundamental concerns. This calls for a renewed emphasis on value education, for philosophical examination of strengths and weaknesses — for critical probings into the aesthetics of music.

That the study of aesthetics is largely neglected in the education of music teachers is both regrettable and paradoxical. Too often the educator tends to regard aesthetic (as well as philosophical) inquiry either as a tedious and quarrelsome rehash of classical and scholastic arguments or as an esoteric discussion having little "down to earth" substance. On the other hand, the teacher of music refers freely to his particular field of endeavor as "aesthetic," or simply as that which deals with the "beautiful." He nobly defends the musical arts on grounds rooted in "aesthetic experiences." Yet, when confronted by students, by administrators, and by the lay public with the task of elucidating on the practice he preaches, he undergoes understandable difficulty.

Just what are our beliefs concerning the nature and value of the musical arts? On what bases are these beliefs derived? What do we *mean* by "good music" and "good taste?" The problems of why, what, and how music should be taught are inherently bound in meaningful answers to such questions.

The controversial reaction to the 1964 Report of the Yale Seminar on Music Education serves to highlight the urgency of existing problems in music education which are, by and large, problems of aesthetics. It seems odd that, of the varied output of texts and general writings dealing with matters of aesthetic concern, very little significant material has been submitted by music educators. Yet the problem of extending and broadening the horizons of the masses toward aesthetic musical understanding remains largely in the province of education. "The way to genuine appreciation of art is thru education. Not the violent simplification of art, but the training of the capacity for aesthetic judgment is the means by which the constant monopolizing of art by a small minority can be prevented." [1]

Contemporary educational questions coupled with unprecedented developments in support of the arts have stimulated new interest in mass needs for aesthetic understanding. While endorsing the arts as essential to a well-balanced society, The Rockefeller Panel Report states that: ". . . the arts are not for a privileged few but for the many, . . . their place is not on the periphery of society but at its center, . . . they are not just a form of recreation but are of central importance to our well being and happiness." [2]

---

[1] Arnold Hauser, *The Social History of Art,* New York: Alfred A. Knopf, Volume II, 1952, p. 959.

[2] Rockefeller Panel Report on the Future of Theatre, Dance, Music in America, *The Performing Arts — Problems and Prospects,* New York: McGraw-Hill Book Co., 1965, pp. 11-12. Used by permission.

The role of music education in uplifting musical tastes and in stimulating artistic integrity has reached a significant level of concern. Philosophical concepts and educational objectives must be re-examined and renewed with aesthetic conviction.

The fact that educators are generally uninformed about philosophy and aesthetics points to the "almost systematic neglect of philosophy and whole realms of aesthetic value in the teacher education program in music";[3] and consequently, in the actual practice of music education. The importance of this book rests on this consideration as well as upon the self-searching needs and professional standards of the music educator in an effort to understand the aesthetic, to identify with the practical, and to speculate with the potential. As a result the music educator should be in a better position to use aesthetic inquiry as a source of ideas and as a logical tool for sorting out values.

To understand the problems of aesthetics, this book probes into the theoretical components of musical aesthetics and educational philosophy. To identify with the practical, pertinent problems in music education are selected for critical analysis. To speculate with the potential, an interpretation of desirable foundations of aesthetic music education is suggested.

Some of the questions which form the core of inquiry are:

1. What is implied by the study of aesthetics and why is it necessary?

2. What is the nature and meaning of the aesthetic experience in music?

3. What are the major theories of aesthetic value and how are these manifested in both educational philosophy and practice?

4. How does the theoretical study of aesthetics aid in the clarification and solution to problems in music education?

5. What are the social, political, and cultural forces which tend to affect desirable goals in aesthetic taste and expression? What of the role of education in such concerns?

If these questions, as well as others raised here, seem to indicate that the commonly held concept of aesthetics, restricted traditionally to a nebulous search for "beauty," has been bypassed, such is not the case. What is implied is simply that the classic interpretation of aesthetics has been broadened to the extent that more inclusive understandings of socio-musical values and related educational means and ends may be realized. In modern aesthetic theory, socio-cultural factors are interrelated with the philosophical and the psychological in the search for solutions to critical problems.

It is hardly the intention of this book to study the ramifications of aesthetics exhaustively. Rather than being comprehensive, the introductory material in Chapter I is a general orientation to the aesthetic-musical-educational complex.

Chapter II is devoted to a review of major theories in aesthetics and educational philosophy in terms of their interrelationships, comparative value systems, and meanings in music and education.

---

[3] Charles Leonhard, "Research: Philosophy and Esthetics," *Journal of Research in Music Education,* III (Spring, 1955), 24.

Chapter III is a critical discussion of aesthetic factors as these pertain to contemporary music education. Some practical issues are examined, and means and ends as well as levels of understanding are explored.

In Chapter IV recommendations for foundations, curricula, pedagogy, and additional research are suggested.

The bibliography is extensive to indicate the divergent nature of knowledge necessary for aesthetic inquiry in contemporary music education; to aid the potential researcher in finding pertinent materials; and to provide a comprehensive source of materials for the music educator whose desire for a deeper familiarity with the literature may be stimulated by this book.

Aesthetics: Dimensions for Music Education may be useful as a general source book for the professional music educator; as a class text for graduate courses in the foundations and problems of music education; as supplementary reading for undergraduate classes in music education; as supplementary reading for classes in the aesthetics of music; or as a general reading for educational administrators and teachers who are involved, in any manner, with music education.

It is not the naive intention of this book to provide an ultimate educational scheme of musical values and practices to serve as terminal goals. It is hoped, however, that it will disturb complacent attitudes and generate significant changes toward the realization of more meaningful programs of aesthetically-centered music education.

I would like to express my gratitude to the many colleagues and students whose probing conversations and class discussions fostered the preparation of this book. Acknowledgements must also be extended to Isaac Thut (University of Connecticut) and to Theodore Brameld (Boston University) for stimulating my interests in philosophy and aesthetics. To Robert Choate (Boston University), for his personal and professional confidence during the past three years, I am most grateful. I am indebted to Bonnie C. Kowall for editorial assistance, and, to my wife for her painstaking criticism and constant patient understanding.

A.A.S.
Rhode Island College
Providence, R. I.

CHAPTER I

AN INTRODUCTION TO AESTHETICS:
MUSIC AND EDUCATION

*T*HE TASK of philosophy is to examine ideas so that certain weaknesses and strengths may be observed, analyzed, and evaluated. The ferment for vital change in a democratic society generates the setting for philosophical struggle — in politics, in theology, in morality, in education, and in the arts.

Our beliefs, feelings, and consequent pleasures derived from music rest on what we determine personally to be of value. Too often we commit ourselves to musical judgments without any substantial reasoning as to why or how conclusions have been reached. What basic criteria guide the music educator in formulating concepts and objectives in philosophy, in curriculum, in teaching methods, or in adapting to cultural change?

To begin with, let us consider the key word *change*. While change in general is often desirable to most music educators, the mere idea provides a pivotal point for argumentation, for inquiry, and for speculation. If education is regarded as an important social agency through which desirable change can be effected, by what reliable standards of value should such changes be determined? Who is to say what musical experiences are best for public school instruction? What kinds of change would be most beneficial to both art and society?

For the music educator the proportions of concern now become significant: Are musical tastes humanistically centered, subject to personal likes and dislikes? Is the student the focal point as the creator of his own musical culture? Is the connoisseur the reliable source of standards rather than preferences of the masses?

There emerges from such questioning a basic conception of dualism — of change and permanence, of absolutism and pragmatism, of traditionalism and liberalism. The cleavages which exist in contemporary music education, primarily because of the plurality of musical values in a changing society, are rooted deeply in aesthetic and philosophical inquiry. To a large extent, research studies in music education have sorely neglected the rational aspects of such discourse. According to Broudy:

> If the facts and scientific theories cannot settle the controversy, and the disputants still wish to continue a rational discussion, they have to pass to another level of argument, namely, the philosophical. Here the disputants defend their value commitments in terms of a theory about what is *really* true, *really* valuable, and *really* real.[1]

The philosophical level of discussion provides a unique control for the imaginative mind and for a most revealing means of examining the manifestations of art as experience. The intrigue that the musical arts have for the general philosopher is quite apparent. Even a cursory examination of the literature shows that the questions of musical meaning, validity, judgment, and significance have drawn the attention of those who may be regarded as intelligent observers of the arts, not directly involved in the affairs of musical production or education. From Plato to Santayana to the present, philosophers have made positive contributions which point up fundamental issues in musical aesthetics and in music education.

With an understandable eagerness for exposing his ideas, the contemporary composer writes, lectures, and demonstrates. He exhibits a growing concern for philosophical and aesthetic validity; he zealously tends to maintain his artistic integrity despite socio-economic pressures; and he is coming to recognize the latent force of mass education as an important catalytic agent in cultural change.

The music educator must approach the task of "music for millions" with comparable enthusiasm. He must help to enable the masses to engage in the philosophical and practical pursuit of worthy musical ends. He must examine his basic beliefs about music, about education, and about aesthetic means and ends.

> ... the best way to maintain the status of music in the curriculum is to preserve its integrity as an art rather than to dissipate its aesthetic potentialities in order to serve non-musical goals, no matter how worthy they may be. ... Let us accept the challenge of this general educator to become convinced of the values that are inherent in music and unique to it, and to maintain them in public education with intense devotion and calculating intelligence.[2]

---

[1] Harry S. Broudy, *Building a Philosophy of Education,* second edition. Englewood Cliffs: Prentice-Hall Inc., 1961, p. 18. Used by permission.

[2] William C. Hartshorn, "Integrity in Music Education," *Music Educators Journal,* 46 (September-October, 1959), 29.

The obvious roles of the music educator — as both musician and teacher — present problems which may be compounded by a variety of psychological subfactors contained within each role. Add to this the social force of mass media, the glamour of musical entertainment, the pressure of a generally uninformed school administration, the limitations of time for instruction, and the problem of humanities in an age of science, and one must agree that the lot of the educator is not an easy one. The problems are real and often frustrating. From day to day the music educator is reminded in some manner of Max Kaplan's observation: How shall we regard the student performer? As the oboe player called Johnny, or Johnny, who happens to play the oboe? An answer favoring either response might be accompanied by a host of supporting ideas ranging from Johnny's needs for social recognition to rather objective considerations for the purity of the musical arts. More likely, "professional" attitudes would prevail, largely in the shape of dogmatic assertions based on specialized interests, egocentric artistic tendencies, and hazy educational arguments.

One fact is clear. No matter what form or direction the argument takes if it involves music education, there will be an inevitable, although inconsistent, reference to matters of aesthetics. To the extent that the nature and meaning of music and music education are derived from and philosophically rooted in aesthetic elements, the results of such study can be rewarding.

Aesthetics — A Branch of Philosophy

It is often surprising for both the musician and the layman to learn that aesthetics is related to general philosophy; that the theoretical problems in aesthetics draw substantially from philosophy in logical procedures as well as in terminology. In general, philosophical discussions revolve about systems of reasoned beliefs that strive for consistency in terms of ontology, epistemology, and axiology — namely, the studies of reality, of truth, and of value. While specific problems in aesthetics are discussed in the study of axiology, relations with the other areas are necessary for a consistency of beliefs.

Philosophy, as applied to the musical arts, may be broadly interpreted then as man's search for the origin, the nature, the criteria, and the cultural manifestations of value in aesthetic expression. Such discussion may involve applied problems (composition, performance, listening experiences, criticism, and education) as well as theoretical problems (criteria for value judgments, i.e., the bases on which musical values and tastes are derived).

The desire for a clarification and meaningful interpretation of ideas constitutes the philosopher's purpose.

For the musician, in general, the study of aesthetics affords a unique opportunity to examine the nature of the musical arts: its meanings, its implied emotionalisms, its effects and values in relation to derived beliefs of reality and of truth. Aesthetics forces a consideration of the latter because of its insistence on consistency. Aesthetics, as such, may not aid the performer to play a particularly involved passage with greater precision, but it should cause the performer to become aware of the significance of his art on a variety of sensitive planes. Musical communication, for example, is an important problem of aesthetics affecting the discriminative sensitivity of every performing musician.

For the music educator the implications of aesthetics are manifested daily in his professional relationships with others, in his actual teaching role, in his concept of the significance of the musical arts, and in his reasoned beliefs in support of formal education as a means of uplifting musical tastes. In short, such study should help us to understand *why* we are doing what we are doing, or what we *ought* to be doing in order to realize other goals.

As philosophy is concerned with principles underlying all knowledge, aesthetics is that branch of speculative philosophy which attempts a broad theoretical description and explanation of the arts and related types of behavior and experience. Aesthetics has been defined as the study of the beautiful, resulting, for example, in the establishment of criteria which would aid one to determine whether and why one particular composition is beautiful while another is not.

The difficulty here lies not only with the narrowness of scope, but also with the interpretation and meaning of the term "beautiful." As Schoen indicates, it is often paradoxical of critics, who do not know what beauty is, to tell others what is or what is not beautiful.[3] However, a definition providing a more inclusive meaning can be found in the *Harvard Dictionary of Music*. According to this source, aesthetics is interpreted as "the study of the relationship of music to the human senses and intellect."

Undoubtedly, if works of art were not spoken or written about, no questions would emerge and no aesthetic problems would exist. Since the reverse is generally true, one discovers that the inclusive study of aesthetics discloses a multiplicity of

---

[3] Max Schoen, "Psychological Problems in Musical Art," *Journal of Research in Music Education,* III (Spring, 1955), 33.

problems which necessitate intensive probing in order to clarify critical positions. Aesthetics may then be regarded further as a philosophy of criticism which functions not on a level of purely sensuous pleasure nor on a level of general approval, but rather on the level of reasoned discrimination. Moreover, although psychological, social, and anthropological data cannot be ignored, a distinction between psychological aesthetics and philosophical aesthetics can be noted. While one deals with the nature of the creative process, and with the aesthetic experience, i.e., the causes and effects of musical works, the other is concerned with questions about the meanings of critical statements relating to artistic values.[4]

Since validity in aesthetic inquiry is dependent upon evidence and substantiation from diverse sources, a broad perspective of interrelationships seems to be most desirable. Considering also the issues in contemporary music education, this point of view is necessary.

To summarize, the aesthetic-musical-educational complex may be analyzed in the following manner. The aesthetic function of music is inherently bound up with the uniqueness of the organization and deliberate control of sound, notated by means of symbols, and characterized by the relationships of music to the human senses and intellect. Man's relationship to music becomes educational when succeeding generations are assisted in becoming critically intelligent about musical styles and forms, about the organization and design of sound, and about the social, emotional, and physical phenomena which characterize music as an art form.

A careful analysis will show that this rather inclusive definition is not as "cold" nor as "intellectual" as it appears at first reading. Because of the broadness of scope in contemporary music education, the directions for aesthetic inquiry are far-reaching. Primarily, it should be recognized that the term "music education" no longer applies to the conventional boundaries of public school music. Both formal and informal aspects, school and community contacts, and public media of communication must also be included. Consider, for example, the ramifications of radio and television on the taste and discrimination of the nation. What is the role of formal education in relation to these channels of informal teaching?

---

[4] Monroe C. Beardsley, *Aesthetics: Problems in the Philosophy of Criticism.* New York: Harcourt, Brace and Co., 1958, pp. 6-7.

The definition also implies that a level of critical intelligence about music is desirable as an educational outcome. To what extent can this be determined or measured? What is expressly meant by the musically educated person? Is it not possible for the private teacher, who also hails from a revered line of tradition, to accomplish the mission of public education? If so, then what is the need for music education in tax-supported schools?

Implied also are matters of extra-musical concern: of education and entertainment, of great and lesser music, of teacher preparation, and indeed, of the need for change itself. These problems affect all aspects of music and education in some manner. According to the professional literature, the solutions are imbedded in a critical redefinition of ends and means, guided by aesthetic considerations. While this, in itself, is sufficient reason to study aesthetics, there are other marked justifications.

Aesthetics will no more teach us how to write poetry than how to build houses. But it may teach us something of what it is that we hear in music or see in buildings or enjoy in our own everyday surroundings. It should inform us through abstraction and analysis as to how the external world as immediate presentation is constituted, by nature itself or by artists. . . . And if we wish to mark ourselves off as human and not merely natural, it is as aesthetic beings that we are best characterized, being capable of enjoying the aesthetic of the world.[5]

The Functions of Aesthetic Inquiry

The study of aesthetics utilizes and synthesizes information from various disciplines, and makes critical application to beliefs concerning the nature and value of art. Experimental psychology, for example, does not attempt to resolve aesthetic disagreements nor to examine values critically. It is not uncommon for the psychologist to become statistically involved in the measurement of emotional responses to individual tones, colors, and chords in isolation from a musical whole. The social scientist may examine the musical behavior of society and analyze objectively its changing dynamics. But rarely is his research expected to produce ideas for desirable change, for musical betterment, or for critical application. Understandably, other fields of study function in a similar manner — economics, political science, cultural anthropology, acoustics, and to a substantial extent, musicology and ethnomusicology. Each has its particular, definitive niche of inquiry relative to the study of music, yet none applies derived knowledge to meanings of "good" or "great," to the development

---

[5] D. W. Prall, *Aesthetic Analysis*. New York: Thomas Y. Crowell Co., 1936, p. 30.

of discriminative techniques, or to the reasons why certain musical beliefs are nurtured. Finally, none of these specialties consciously comes to grips with educational problems and possibilities for solution. Yet all of these fields of study remain in the province of aesthetic inquiry which uniquely draws evidence and directions from other areas of knowledge for the purpose of substantiating or altering artistic beliefs.

Although aesthetic understanding demands intimate experience with art, it has been argued that the study of aesthetics causes musical vitality and interest to wane. Such an assumption lacks intellectual substance. The ambiguity of our subjectively conceived likes and dislikes often requires a certain amount of objective evidence to lend credulity to beliefs about music. Egoistic likes and dislikes are often misleading and musically irresponsible. Aesthetic study not only sharpens interest in the musical arts, but also tends to point up questionable differences between such knotty matters as "liking" in relation to "valuing." Questions of musical meaning, of listening responses, of musical creativity, of education and entertainment, are all aesthetic questions. The study of aesthetics, therefore, helps to quicken intellectual and emotional curiosities, to foster the need for empirical evidence in differentiating between intrinsic and extrinsic values of music, and to develop critical attitudes and extended interest in all phases of musical behavior.

Traditionally, the responsibility for teaching aesthetics remains with the professor of philosophy in the liberal arts college. But while musical studies in history, theory, and education generally tend to bypass the aesthetic dimensions for the practical, the area of musical aesthetics is often a special problem to the professor of philosophy. His admitted lack of musical skills may prevent him from treating the aesthetics of music with the vigor he allots to the other arts.

To be utilized effectively, aesthetic theory must be applied to musical concepts. This means that every class in music (at any level of instruction) is also a class in the aesthetics of music. An educational goal of musical discrimination requires a process which is both sequential and developmental, involving experiences in aesthetic interaction which proceed from the simple and obvious to the more complex and abstract. To realize this the teacher of music must understand the means and ends of aesthetic education.

The inclusion or exclusion of any facet of the instructional program is of prime concern. Serious consideration must be given to the validity of any curricular practice which interferes with or seriously impedes aesthetic goals. Aesthetically-centered music education requires a critical concern for those extra-musical forces which tend to influence worthy goals — socially, economically, politically, morally, and psychologically. The reliance on personal prestige, on isolated musical skills, on overspecialization, on entertainment factors, and on selective education for the talented indicate deficiencies in aesthetic understandings and lean towards narrow educational results.

Other problem areas which invite aesthetic inquiry include specialization and general music, contests and festivals, the self-contained classroom, the marching and stage bands, required music in high school, standards of musical literature for both performance and listening, pedagogical techniques in teaching for "appreciation," and the educational obligations to new and experimental music. By reducing issues to aesthetic components, we learn that much of what is commonly accepted as musical truth, as musical reality, and as musical value, is in many instances ambivalent, standing in dire need of scientific, historical, and cultural validity. The antitheses involving the nature of musicality and the musical experience, iconographic and symbolistic meanings, objective and subjective values, the nature of the creative process, the presumed universality of music as a language, social and individual manifestations of musical value, criteria for formal musical criticism, and their function in terms of education — all tend to remain in the province of aesthetic inquiry.

The Aesthetic Experience

Some form of communication occurs whenever there is contact with a musical event, whether in the rehearsal room, in the concert hall, in the dentist's office, or in the bus terminal. The descriptions of such events are often quite vague. And the derived "values" are usually explained on the basis of some non-artistic idea. As an illustration, some of the general purposes for recorded listening experiences in the elementary school have been stated as follows: "to calm noisy, excited children; to stimulate inattentive, sleepy children; to provide music for quiet listening." [6]

Aside from the fact that these purposes lack the validity of research and point to utilitarian (or therapeutic) ends, they are nevertheless labeled by their proponents as aesthetic. Surely a

------

[6] These are but three among others actually listed in a current school catalog and endorsed by a music educator.

deeper insight is necessary in order to avoid both careless usage of aesthetic meanings and questionable educational purposes. In this section, therefore, we shall explore some ideas about the aesthetic experience which bear on our definition of aesthetics and on musical and educational implications.

The aesthetic experience occurs as a result of an interaction between a particular subject (a listener, for example) and a given object (the particular musical work). During this interaction, musical beliefs and understandings are applied, enjoyable moments and disappointments are noted, and critical judgments are voiced.

This subject-object involvement is fundamental, since music cannot in itself be aesthetic. The composer's initial creation, the performer's sensitive rendition (or re-creation), and the listener's capacity for musical reception are all keenly interwoven in an intricate process of aesthetic perception — an intellectual and emotional adventure with a musical event. The outcome (although dependent upon a number of factors) will be influenced strongly by two basic considerations: (a) The inherent quality and intrinsic interest of the musical composition; that is, its potential, and (b) The musical background of the listener, his preparation, experience, interest, attention span; in brief, the subject's conditioned attitude and behavior.

Accordingly, some educational experiences may be considered merely as preparations for a musically aesthetic experience. The necessary drilling on isolated choral or instrumental parts, the introduction by means of pictures and sounds to orchestral instruments, or the isolated practice on a second clarinet part are all preparations for some higher (aesthetic) end. Hence, the consummation of such isolated experiences is realized in some form of culminating experience which should, if properly guided, be rich in aesthetic interest.[7]

The values of aesthetic interaction cannot be measured in terms of our basic needs for food, clothing, or shelter. Nor is there any sound validity in the moral, social, or political thought which would claim utilitarian or practical benefits on aesthetic grounds.

The aesthetic experience is unique in that it seeks no utilitarian fulfillment in the future. Unlike the practical experience of banking, of daily toil, or of visiting the dentist, the aesthetic ex-

---

[7] Max Kaplan has compared the intensive rehearsal schedule of an orchestra with that of a military organization, in that both are preparing for the significant future event, i.e., the real moment of combat, the "actual" performance.

perience exists for its own purposes. While the aesthetic experience can symbolize and enrich the realm of practical activity, it constantly questions any suggested or direct referential relationship. It seeks to give new and varied interpretation of the human drama, yet its meanings are often misconceived as mere escapes from life's involvements. It reminds us that "man cannot live by bread alone," and at the same time disparages concepts compressed into slogans. Those people who are too busy with daily practical matters to understand the values of aesthetic involvement may have little regard for the aesthetic experience either for themselves or for others. We can observe many levels of approach to the aesthetic experience in most cross-sections of society. The practical-minded educational administrator (basically he must be) who is artistically deficient (he need not be) will often commit the error of identifying the practical with the aesthetic. To him music in the schools exists for functional reasons. Those purposes listed at the beginning of this section would be quite acceptable in his philosophy. Only when college entrance examination boards include a part on musical information, will his practical nature motivate him to provide for these studies in the program of general education.

From just this brief discussion, we may assume that the aesthetic experience is a complex affair involving more than the search for the soothing musical moment. The fact that musical backgrounds, philosophical beliefs and attitudes vary so, introduces the problems of a plurality of views all offering explanations of the aesthetic experience. During any one musical performance, for instance, the experience of the conductor may differ somewhat from the experience of those who are either performing or listening (not to mention the variety of experiences from performer to performer or from listener to listener).

This plurality of responses, while sometimes difficult to make meaningful, need not introduce frustrating reactions. Artistic inquiry thrives on a sharing of views, on a strengthening of one's own beliefs by questioning others, or on a revision (or conversion) to a more acceptable set of beliefs. In other words, the aesthetic experience cannot be guided to its maturity like a well-detailed recipe. In modern theory, however, the desire for a more meaningful understanding of the aesthetic experience has stimulated the need for education. Reliance on information from diverse fields has become essential. The classroom and general school community could provide excellent situations for aesthetic inquiry and for the development of aesthetic attitudes.

Our discussion has indicated some of the difficulties in formulating any one concrete notion which would clarify the meaning of the aesthetic experience. The major cause of difficulty can be explained in one way by the changing dynamics of art and society.

Throughout all history and up to the present day, art has been explained and valued in nonaesthetic terms. It has been esteemed for its social utility, or because it inculcates religious beliefs, or because it makes men moral, or because it is a source of knowledge. In all such cases . . . art is valued for the consequences to which it gives rise, not for its intrinsic interest. In recent centuries, however, there has been much greater emphasis upon the aesthetic significance of art.[8]

If we apply Stolnitz's view of the nonaesthetic to some common practices in music education, then it must be admitted that much of what does occur is highly questionable. Consider the annual graduation exercise: Is not the music for this occasion (processionals, recessionals, and the familiar "selection") chosen primarily from a functional point of view? This is not to imply that this type of musical experience is "bad," or uneducational (for all involved), but merely that it tends to be nonaesthetic. In lieu of an exciting subject-object involvement, the subject's attention is misdirected, and the music played usually (often, necessarily) contains little intrinsic interest. The argument would hold even if the music were selected with most careful judgment; for to be considered aesthetic (according to our meaning here) the listener must be in total communication with the musical event, not with the particular occasion.

The aesthetic experience requires a concentrated direction of attention centered in the musical object. The development of habits of attentive listening is therefore an important goal for music education. The uniqueness of music as an art, characterized by tonal and temporal dimensions, places serious demands on the subject. Among other considerations, sensitive hearing is dependent upon familiarity with formal organization, an adequate musical memory, a precise awareness of details, a discriminating attitude of attention, and a relevancy of musical knowledge. The last two — attitude and relevance — are rather primary characteristics of the aesthetic experience and deserve further attention.

---

[8] Jerome Stolnitz, *Aesthetics and Philosophy of Art Criticism: A Critical Introduction.* Boston: Houghton Mifflin Co., 1960, p. 31.

Stolnitz defines the aesthetic attitude as "disinterested and sympathetic attention to and contemplation of any object of awareness for its own sake." [9] Not to be confused with uninterested, the word *disinterested* refers to a selective mode of attention to the object, not for ulterior or functional purposes, but for "the purpose of just having the experience." Our interest, then, must be focused on the musical event, not in any passing manner (such a manner may be involved in listening for the purpose of merely passing judgment) but in an intensely involved and isolated concentration. A disinterested attitude is needed by the subject in order to communicate with the object without interferences of a practical nature. Sympathetic refers to the means by which preparation for a discriminative response is brought about.

When we apprehend an object aesthetically, we do so in order to relish its individual quality, whether the object be charming, stirring, vivid, or all of these. If we are to appreciate it, we must accept the object "on its own terms." We must make ourselves receptive to the object and "set" ourselves to accept whatever it may offer to perception. We must therefore inhibit any responses which are "un-sympathetic" to the object which alienate us from it or are hostile to it. [10]

Conditioned feelings — religious, moral, and political — may inhibit aesthetic contact. Listeners, for example, who regard electronic music as aseptic or dehumanized on the grounds of traditionally conceived values, find it difficult to focus attention at such presentations. Similarly, non-Christians often find it difficult to assume disinterested attitudes during interactions with music which is predominantly Christian in character.

Children's concerts by civic symphony orchestras have become major events in many communities. These concerts, financed by private and public funds, are usually carefully arranged and presented as rare musical opportunities for school youth. Following one of these concerts, a fifth grader was asked what he enjoyed most. His answer was swift and to the point, "The bus ride to the auditorium." This common occurrence points up aesthetic deficiencies in the development of both disinterested and sympathetic attitudes. Surely these children need more than mere exposure to music.

Other incidents, more profound in scope, serve as reminders of the variety of deeply imbedded subjectivisms which may inhibit the listener from complete immersion in the aesthetic ex-

---

[9] *Ibid.,* p. 35.
[10] *Ibid.,* p. 36.

perience. Personal dislike for a composer's non-musical egocentricities and beliefs could conceivably carry over into the listener's attitude. Can we successfully separate the man from his music in the aesthetic experience? The extent to which such attitudes have caused consistent cultural errors in socio-political history is of no minor concern.

Factors that influence and limit attitudes in the aesthetic experience may emerge from social or educational conditioning — personal beliefs about the social mores of art ("Jazz has its place, but . . ."); conservative or narrow musical tastes ("Now Tchaikovsky, there's a composer! These 'moderns' like Debussy and Stravinsky, just do nothing for me . . ."); deficiencies in musical listening ("Admittedly, I am musically ignorant, but I know what I like, and have a right to my opinion"); notions concerning the affective qualities of music ("I like music because it relaxes me . . . but this twelve-tone music is disturbing and ugly — the composer must be demented . . .").

While Stolnitz's notion of "disinterestedness" may appear impersonal, it still remains that a certain detachment or centering of attentive attitude is basic to the aesthetic experience and to musical understanding.[11]

The matter of aesthetic relevance is also selective in that it makes constant reference to the object itself. Knowledge about a particular musical work or period must not remain external to the music itself. But such knowledge must be learned and made relevant to the aesthetic object.

The teacher cannot assume either that the student will do this for himself, or that the role of education is merely to transmit the "facts" about art. By focusing attention on the musical object, the student should be directed to analyze and to utilize learned information through frequent hearings, so that the vague may become clear. The centering on musical materials is essential to the educational and aesthetic process. The reliance on story associations (mostly unauthenticated), as well as iconographic representations tend to detract from, rather than add to, the relevance of the music itself. At best these activities serve some function as motivational procedures. Finger-painting to the accompaniment of Debussy's *Afternoon of a Faun*, as well as a description of Handel's financial difficulties in running opera companies, are both examples of problems in aesthetic relevance.

---

[11] For a variation of this view see Jerome Schiller, "An Alternative to Aesthetic Disinterestedness," *Journal of Aesthetics and Art Criticism*, 22 (Spring, 1964), 295-302.

While both are interesting, they are nevertheless irrelevant to an understanding of the musical art of Debussy or Handel. Central to the teaching of music should be the standpoint of the composer and the artistic product, rather than irrelevant details and questionable experiences.[12]

It has been argued that purely technical involvement in music frequently causes the aesthetic experience to become cold and shallow in meaning. To some extent, this cannot be denied. A narrow objective attitude, in which the mere technicalities of music govern the listener's attitude, can act as a deterrent to aesthetic perception. Pitch deficiencies, rhythmic irregularities, as well as too much vibrato may cause a keen listener to lose interest. The aesthetically mature musician, however, while involved technically, as a matter of training, will strive for an experience which would involve the sum total of his perceptive resources. This is especially true during the auditing of newer works when recall, familiarity of style, and conditioned attitudes towards consonance and dissonance, for example, are intermingled in a critical aesthetic interaction. When asked for a value judgment after such an experience, this listener might state that he is somewhat uncertain, that repeated hearings would be necessary, or that a familiarity with the score would be more desirable. Such an experience has all the earmarks of being aesthetic in spite of its obvious uncertainty. Aesthetic "enjoyment," therefore, is a growing, progressive process which may not be completely fulfilled with one experience. In fact, the nature of the musical arts is such that it requires frequent repetition, and careful analytical judgment for significant meanings of artistic validity to emerge. The history of première performances confirms this assumption.

Dewey's observations concerning aesthetic relevance indicate that a narrow atomistic attitude based on mere technical proficiency could conceivably act as a stumbling block in the aesthetic experience:

To look at a work of art in order to see how well certain rules are observed and canons conformed to impoverishes perception. But to strive to note the ways in which certain conditions are fulfilled, such as the organic means by which the media is made to express and carry definite parts, or how the problem of an adequate individualization is solved, sharpens perception and enriches its content.[13]

[12] Charles Rosen, "The Proper Study of Music," *Perspectives of New Music*, I (Fall-Winter, 1962), 80-88.

[13] John Dewey, *Art as Experience*. New York: Putnam's & Coward-McCann, 1959, p. 205.

Dewey's pragmatic conception of the aesthetic experience maintains the necessary role of intelligent behavior. The attitudes of both the artist and the listener are thus inherently involved. While the former normally projects his efforts with the listener in mind, the latter must create his own experiences comparable to those of the composer.

The resulting mixture of emotionalism and artistic communication depends, therefore, on the extent to which composer, performer, and listener exert mutual efforts. In this manner, the intellectual observation of the canonic bases for Bach's *Two-Part Inventions* will not impoverish perception; an analytic understanding of the rows used in Schoenberg's *Wind Quintet* will not detract from the music. On the contrary, both help to enrich the actual musical experience and both point up the listener's need for creative problem-solving.

While emotions serve psychologically as creative drives, which manifest themselves characteristically in qualitative symbols (sound, in the case of music), it is the aesthetic need which explains the detachment and plasticity of these qualities from the "ordered-world of cause-effect relations." [14] Qualities previously neutral in worth (the isolated chord, tone row, canon, etc.) become artistic totalities — objects of aesthetic value — through the composing personality. The aesthetic experience should not be regarded then as a piddling luxury or an escape from life's involvements, but as a singular means by which the nature of the creative individual and the source of creative urges can be explored. Irrelevancies and externalities present a constant source of problems. While they cannot be ignored they must be dealt with on a conscious intellectual plane.

There is considerable agreement that the attitudinal and relevant factors of aesthetic experience are not founded on universal responses in tonal materials, but acquired through education. Proof for this lies in the tendency for the trained listener to objectify musical meanings (to explain in technical terms) and the untrained listener to subjectify (to explain in sensuous terms). In other words, if the aesthetic experience occurs as an interaction between the listener and the musical work, the value of the experience depends on both the preparation of the subject to perceive and the intrinsic value of the object to yield. It is in the cultivation of desirable attitudes, of experience through interaction with aesthetic (and by way of comparison, nonaesthetic) objects, that

---

[14] Ralph J. Hallman, "Aesthetic Motivation in the Creative Arts," *Journal of Aesthetics and Art Criticism*, 23 (Summer, 1965), 453-459.

education makes its contribution. The paramount task for music education is not only to nurture the improvement of taste and discrimination, but also to develop the latent aesthetic reasons or criteria for such behavior.

A keen awareness of artistic details enriches the aesthetic experience and requires perceptive attention characterized by activity rather than passivity. Such activity gives organized meaning and substance to what otherwise might be a mere outpouring of pleasant or unpleasant sound. In this way we "live" the music as it progresses, both emotionally and intellectually. The luxury of reviewing isolated phrases or episodes for purposes of musical analysis is not permitted within the temporal limitations of a given musical event. The development of an acute awareness of details, of structural concerns, of style, of symbolic allusions, of necessary skills, of habits, attitudes, and irrelevancies can be learned. Accompanied by rich activities in making music, listening to music, criticizing music, and as a result, enjoying music, an aesthetic approach can be an exciting way to study. The educational function of music must be conceived in the belief that aesthetic stimulation is a necessary facet of life, that musical tastes can be developed and improved, and that experiences in music should be aesthetically oriented.

Problems in Aesthetic Significance

The ability to respond aesthetically to music depends to a considerable extent upon one's ability to assume a disinterested attitude and upon one's capacity to discriminate factors of musical relevance. Both manifest themselves in formulated beliefs concerning the significance of art in general.

If the aesthetic experience involves an interaction between subject and object, then nothing is aesthetic or nonaesthetic in itself. In other words, music cannot exist in an aesthetic sense, as an isolated phenomenon in the composer's studio. A social interaction is both desirable and necessary. The culmination of such interaction rests in the value judgments, feeling responses, and emotionalities expressed about the experience. In a sense we verbalize our reactions in some statement pointing to what we can call artistic significance. Artistic significance depends upon the sum total of complex ideas and personal beliefs that culminate in a theory of art: the role of the composer, performer, and consumer; the process of artistic creation; some definitive view of the activity of art as opposed to more random processes of life; the psychological bases for conditioned musical expectations and responses; and insight into the motivic, affective, attitudinal, and objective theories that guide personal feelings about art and its relation to the human intellect and feelings.

Artistic significance in the aesthetic experience is most important when art rather than nature is involved.

Art is a creative activity carried on by human beings, whereas nature by definition is not. Hence, art has social significance which nature lacks. Furthermore, works of art are almost always stable and enduring and they can be readily copied or reproduced. Hence, they usually can be shared.[15]

The complexities and subtleties inherent in the musical object, for example, require a sensitive feeling and knowing of details which would not be necessary when observing interesting cloud formations. In the latter experience, technical training may interfere with aesthetic perception; in the former, properly directed, it would tend to enhance perception.

Aesthetic theories of artistic significance are rather involved because of the complex nature of art. Solutions to knotty questions are not easily found. For example, how can we estimate the extent to which moral, philosophical, and religious prejudices have prevented Western man from an unobstructed view of art? When we criticize a musical work are we not talking about some particular production of it, rather than the work in general? If the experience, musical or otherwise, is one of "terror," can it also be aesthetically "good?" In what ways do our conditioned likes and dislikes tend to become standards? Is the function of silence also an integral part of the musically aesthetic experience?[16] If music is commonly conceived of as a universal language, why do we experience such difficulty in understanding the nuances of Oriental music? Is there any meaningful aesthetic relation between the genesis of a work and the completed work itself? To what extent can moral overtones in music be really recognized? What makes music "religious?" Does the visual factor in musical performance enhance or detract from a sensitive aesthetic experience? Does the composer's genius have a divine origin? What would be the possible reasons for the aesthetic experience to occur negatively? What is the role of education considering the varying standards of artistic significance?

---

[15] Stolnitz, op. cit., p. 47.

[16] See Zofia Lissa, "Aesthetic Functions of Silence and Rest in Music," The Journal of Aesthetics and Art Criticism, 22 (Summer, 1964), 443-453; also John Cage, Silence. Wesleyan University Press, 1961.

To be sure, this sampling can mature into an overwhelming list. Each question stimulates a pointed line of inquiry which bears on the other in the search for truth. As futile as this may seem, aesthetic inquiry is nevertheless crucial to a rational understanding of the arts in contemporary society.

The arguments and debates of aestheticians, the experiments and theories of psychologists, and the speculations of musicologists and composers still continue and are ample indication that the problem of musical meaning and communication are with us today. In fact, the inclusion of music as a part of liberal education, the unpatronizing and serious consideration given to non-Western music, and the attempts to include the art of music in studies dealing with cultural history have made the problems more pressing.[17]

The need for more intensive probing into the aesthetic experience in general and its musical implications in particular has also become more pressing in view of greater concerns over artistic significance.

Though seeming accident is a delight, we believe that real accident is foreign to good art. Without this basic belief the listener would have no reason for suspending judgment, revising opinion, and searching for relationships; the divergent, the less probable, the ambiguous would have no meaning. There would be no progression, only change. Without faith in the purposefulness and rationality of art, listeners would abandon their attempts to understand, to reconcile deviants to what has come before, or to look for their *raison d'être* in what is still to come.[18]

Langer indicates further that aesthetic inquiry has risen to new heights because of new ideas concerning knowledge. No longer can such contemplation remain isolated in the realm of classical philosophy, for "to construct the conceptual framework of knowledge . . . one has to know the difficulties, paradoxes, and mysteries of the subject." [19]

According to Dewey the musical arts represent a human need, creative expressions of activity and experience. The aesthetic experience, therefore, reflects and imbues with new meaning the struggle-fulfillment rhythm of practical experience. It is man's rationality that enables him to perceive this relation during the experience. The fulfillment of aesthetic pleasure occurs when effective communication takes place. The need for musical ex-

---

[17] Leonard B. Meyer, *Emotion and Meaning in Music*. Chicago: University of Chicago, 1956, p. ix.

[18] *Ibid.*, p. 75.

[19] Suzanne K. Langer, editor, *Reflections on Art*. Baltimore: Johns Hopkins Press, 1958, p. xii.

pression is unique, simply because words cannot adequately express the human range of feelings, emotions, and ideas.

New psychological, physiological, and sociological factors concerning the effects of tone on human responsiveness provide data which de-emphasize other-worldly concepts of music and strengthen the consideration that music as a symbolic art is rooted in the rhythm of ordinary experience. The matter and form of music, norm-deviant patterns, stress-release complexes, the dissonance-consonance relationships, cadential effects, tonal and atonal elements — are all made vivid in the personal experiences of the active listener, who symbolically and apperceptively transfers musical meanings to and from the arena of ordinary experience.

To perceive, a beholder must create his own experience . . . comparable to those the original producer underwent. The one who is too lazy, idle, or indurated in convention to perform this work will not see or hear. His "appreciation" will be a mixture of scraps of learning with conformity to norms of conventional admiration and with confused, even if genuine emotional excitation.[20]

The need for active perception, for a strong involvement of the ordinary and the aesthetic is stressed also by Hauser.

What can art signify to one who does not judge it from a position in real life, who is not entangled in life as deeply, as passionately as the artist himself! Art helps those who seek her help, coming to her with their qualms of conscience, their doubts, and their prejudices. Dumb to the dumb, she can speak only to those who question her.[21]

Detailed analyses of the literature reveal a growing tendency to explain the nature and meaning of music in terms of more humanistic, cultural realities. The rather mundane outlook toward the functions of music as a mere gratification of the senses is being supplanted by broader interests in creative essences. In lieu of direct sensuous pleasure then is the subtle yet critical concern for artistic significance.

The very complexity of the musical arts indicates the difficulties in assuming any one universal notion concerning significance. Freudian explanations of creative impulses, Darwinian theories of survival value, Helmholtz's assumption of pleasurable sensations, Platonic views of the morality and ethics of music, Soviet socialist realism, Seashore's theories of self-expression, Meyer's psychology of the norm-deviant relationship, Croce's

---

[20] Dewey, op. cit., p. 54.
[21] Arnold Hauser, The Philosophy of Art History. New York: Alfred A. Knopf, 1959, p. 40.

idealistic concept of intuition, and Langer's hypothesis of logical symbolic expression — all offer strong, but divergent interpretations.

Vigorous emphases on the social nature of music have risen in opposition to the puristic concept of art for art's sake. The purist, for example, would hold that music must conform to an immutable law of artistic adequacy, that music is an isolated art, distinctly separated from life's involvements. Values, and hence artistic significance, are to be found solely in the formal organization of musical devices. The medium of music does not permit storytelling for imitative associations. What is required of the listener is merely formal technical knowledge which constitutes the structural organization. To seek explanations beyond this is to remove oneself from the aesthetic experience. Accordingly, the purist believes that music is superior as an art form, for its nonrepresentational qualities are divorced from ordinary experience and possess a unique character in an isolated field of endeavor. Although purist theories supported by Bell, Fry, Pater, Hanslick, and others are historically later developments than imitative and emotive ones, the issues they introduce are nevertheless important. The fact that so many contemporary composers support purist theories enhances the objective approach and prevents us from disregarding the concept of art for art's sake.

Philosophy in general aids the individual and the group by studying questions that enlarge conceptions of the possible, enrich intellectual imagination, and diminish dogmatic assurances. Aesthetics, a branch of philosophy and psychology, helps us not only to analyze works of art in order to understand their significance, but also to make critical judgments on their value. The problems which one encounters in aesthetic inquiry are, for the most part, those of the aesthetic experience and artistic significance. The theoretical conflict involves, essentially, a fundamental dichotomy of purist and expressionist beliefs.

Music education is inherently involved with aesthetic education. The problems, means, and ends of both are mutually related. The task of extending and broadening the musical horizon of the masses toward aesthetic values remains, finally, in the province of education. Is this function unique for contemporary education? Are there indications in past history of aesthetic problems? Of educational involvements? Considering the changing interrelationships of music, education, and aesthetics what can we learn from the past as guides for the present? These questions form the hub of the final section in this introductory chapter.

Some Historical Outlooks

The word — aesthetics — was first used in 1735 by Alexander B. Baumgarten in relation to the study of sensuous experience as opposed to the logical sciences. During the late eighteenth and nineteenth centuries, such distinctions became the hub of various theories. By the twentieth century, the study of aesthetics was well established on artistic and philosophical, as well as scientific levels. The conflicts over autonomous and heteronomous values have emerged coincidentally with the social history of the musical arts. Among the most illustrative eras of history when the problems of music, aesthetics, and education reached significant heights was the period of classical antiquity.

In early Greece, the governing classes exercised their political controls in artistic censorship. The theatre was considered an instrument of propaganda. Contrary to the modern view, which sets the artist above his work, the ancient world revered the creation and subordinated the creator. In classical Athens, art was still mere handicraft and the artist a craftsman. Problems of increased leisure time and the "good" life were important to the Greek philosophers just as such socio-aesthetic problems are prevalent today.[22]

The metaphysical theories of Plato provided the philosophical basis for a system of musical aesthetics which regarded art as imitation and stressed the emotional and ethical mores of Greek antiquity. Since art reflected emotions and ideas connected with the paramount ethos and institutions of social life, and since a change from Dorian to Lydian mode, for example, might promote civic degeneration, Plato condoned a censorship of the musical arts.

Plato's musical aesthetics began by attributing moral characteristics to the Greek modes, and evolved into "systematic descriptions of the materials and patterns of musical compositions."[23] The concepts of ethos and pathos, of Appolonian morality and Dionysian sensuousness, of classical and romantic tendencies, thus emerged in Plato's metaphysical philosophy synthesizing the musical aesthetics of the ancient East and West. In Plato's idealistic philosophy music was viewed as an art of abstract imitation echoing the universal values of virtue and morality. Music education for the Athenians provided an effective means for inculcating a spiritual essence of the good.

---

[22] Arnold Hauser, *The Social History of Art*, Vol. I. New York: Alfred A. Knopf, 1951, pp. 1-115.

[23] Donald J. Grout, *A History of Western Music*. New York: W. W. Norton and Co., 1960, p. 7.

A child thus exposed to the proper musical modes would unconsciously develop discriminating habits and abilities which would allow him to distinguish good from evil. After music had moulded the character of the child and made him emotionally stable, the study of philosophy would reveal to him in full consciousness the highest knowledge.[24]

Not only music education, but also such matters as musical innovations and artistic license were regarded as politically important. But it should not be overlooked that Plato's concern was culturally oriented to the welfare of the Greek State and to his admiration for the rigidness of Spartan philosophy.

In Plato's *Republic* ("Parable of the Cave"), as well as in *The Meno*, the philosophical bases for mimesis and education are clarified. The metaphysical dualism of both a spiritual and material realm of ideas is transcendental in essence. That is, the soul or mind which possesses innate knowledge (of the "perfect" music, for example), is cloaked during life, but returns to the spiritual realm after death in its eternal seeking for the good. In other words, the body is mortal, living in the material realm of sense experience, while the soul, in an eternal state, dwells in the spiritual realm of ideas. The role of education in effecting a satisfactory recall of ideas is most significant.

In Plato's view, education is confined to the recapitulation of truth already known. All genuine knowledge is innate, having been derived from observing or contemplating pure being in the world of the ideal; that is to say, it belongs to the structure of the mind itself. Knowledge, therefore, is fixed and unchangeable. It consists of photostatic copies of the universal and ideal objects that constitute reality, and these photostatic copies are deposited in the soul itself during its pre-existent life. According to Plato, knowledge neither grows, nor is it created; it is merely recalled.[25]

In Plato's aristocracy, compulsory education is under state control; service to the state is mandatory. Talent and ability are recognized with a provision for the transfer of individuals from one class of society to another. All educational activities are directed to the process by which people in the "gold" class may be discovered, for only these have the capacity to cope with ideas or rather with the recovery of knowledge in the spiritual realm of ideas.

---

[24] Julius Portnoy, *The Philosopher and Music*. New York: The Humanities Press, 1954, p. 15.

[25] Frederick Eby and Charles F. Arrowood, *The History and Philosophy. of Education, Ancient and Medieval*. Englewood Cliffs: Prentice-Hall, Inc., 1940, p. 375. Used by permission.

The influence of Plato on Aristotle is quite evident, for the latter also upheld the notion of music as an imitative art rooted in the mysteries of cosmic harmonies. But beyond this, Aristotle regarded music as emulation, an ideal imitation that stresses the actualizing power of the artist.

Still the ethics of the artist and the morality of the listener were seriously interrelated in matters of censorship and music education. Under Platonic influence, guided by the doctrine of ethos based on the Golden Mean (for example, preference for the Dorian mode as a numerical modal mean), Aristotle developed a philosophy of music education.

Aristotle made it clear at the outset that those who judge music must first be performers with a fair degree of accomplishment themselves. Only those who had a knowledge of the various modes, rhythms and melodies and a technical appreciation of the music which was being performed could first, understand the music, and secondly, evaluate it in order to form a rational judgment of its worth. The Athenian youth must therefore be made musically literate if he was to become an enlightened citizen.[26]

According to the prescriptions of the Golden Mean, overindulgence in musically technical proficiencies for the sake of amusement or for professional competition were rejected. Instruments which required greater skill in performance (such as the flute and harp) were not educationally valid, since the purpose of music education was self-improvement, not a practice of the art. (The latter purpose was not for the freeman, but for the slave or paid performer.)

Although both Plato and Aristotle felt that the ultimate function of music should be the improvement of society, Aristotle's rationalism stimulated a more liberal approach. His theory that the music must not merely imitate, but rather recreate the world of natural sounds into idealized forms, stems from a questioning of the two senses of imitation — mere reflective imitation, which is passive, and creative imitation, which stresses activity (mimesis). Accordingly, music was to be studied for a variety of purposes — for moral purification, for rational criticism, for recreation, as well as for pure enjoyment.

Is it to instruct, to amuse, to employ leisure? Now all these ends are properly allotted to it, for it appears to partake of them all; for play is necessary for relaxation, and relaxation is pleasant, as it is a medicine for that uneasiness which arises from labour. It is admitted that a happy life must be an honorable one, and a pleasant one, too, since happiness consists in both these; and we all agree, that music is

---

[26] Portnoy, *op. cit.*, p. 26.

one of the most pleasing things whether alone or accompanied with a voice.[27]

With Aristoxenus, Aristotle's pupil, the Greek period of musical creativity and Athenian culture drew to a close. The theories of Aristoxenus introduced elements of humanism which transcended the purely moral and mathematical interpretations of Plato. These ideas supported the subjective belief that a true aesthetic of music went beyond the physics and acoustics of sound to culminate in feeling, and implied that man remained the sole judge of what was "good and bad" in music. While Aristoxenus' theories were to lie dormant until the enlightenment of the Renaissance, they did introduce a scientific and psychological view of aesthetic relations and musical criticism rooted in humanism.

Platonic echoes are still heard today in modern aesthetic theories, in practical matters of art, as well as in music education. To know the philosophical and cultural bases of these concepts in the past helps to promote understandings of more recent developments — for example, the political and moral emphases in Soviet music and education.

That musical and educational complexities existed during the Colonial and pre-Colonial periods in America should not be surprising. Together with a great tradition of cultural ideas, we also imported European aesthetics. Interlaced with deep Puritanical feelings for the religious and moral implications of music, the progress of the musical arts was far from dynamic.

The delay in permitting music to enter the portals of formal education may be attributed largely to misconceptions in both musical values and pedagogy. It was more a matter of aesthetic concern than functional need that stimulated Lowell Mason and the Boston School Department in 1838 to experiment with music education. Mason had to prove not only that music could be taught properly in the public schools, but also that the imaginative and affective qualities of music were important educational goals. His argument for music education has been frequently reiterated because of its contemporary implications.

Music is almost the only branch of education aside from divine truth whose direct tendency is to cultivate feeling. Our systems of education generally proceed too much on the principle that we are merely intellectual beings . . . hence we often find the most learned the least agreeable.[28]

---

[27] Aristotle, *Politics,* as quoted in Edward Walford, *The Politics and Economics of Aristotle.* London: George Bell and Sons, 1908, p. 277.

[28] Lowell Mason, *Manual of the Boston Academy of Music.* Boston, Seventh Edition, 1851, pp. 23-24.

European developments in music education did not evolve without comparable cultural and, consequently, aesthetic difficulties. During the Middle Ages the spiritual sway of the clergy upheld a transcendental, metaphysically-oriented outlook. Platonic ideas permeated this theocentric world with new spiritual content. The purpose of music was functional — a means of effecting a closer union between man and God.

> The basic propostion in the philosophy of the Church Fathers was that music is the servant of religion. Only that music is good which, without obtruding its own charms, opens the mind to Christian teachings and disposes the soul to holy thoughts. Music without words cannot do this.[29]

The position of the church towards music education reflected Platonic theories — of preparing the mind for the contemplation of higher truths, and of promoting attitudes of divine contemplation divorced from mundane affairs. The regard for music and religion as "two sides of the same coin" may be summed up in the philosophies of the prophets Amos and Isaiah.

> That music was desirable as an appurtenance of religion, as a means to exalt the soul of the worshipper to new attitudes of piety and righteousness, that the prophet could understand and approve, but music as a provider of pleasure, a titillation of the senses, a luxurious art for art's sake — the idea was to him completely foreign, indeed abominable. Beautiful was music only when it served a higher purpose, the revelation of the word of God; ugly and mean when it served mere sensual delight.[30]

The ideas of artistic inspiration, naturalism, inborn talent, and individualism were the creations of the Renaissance. The new spirit of craftsmanship was coupled by a more intensive interest in art education. Music education became standardized in the court schools and in parochial institutions. It remained the task of the Renaissance artist and composer to suggest the idea of the beautiful in art, justified in itself, to be seen and heard for its own sake.

During the Baroque era music education in Europe was somewhat limited to instruction in performance and composition for aspiring professionals. No public institutional organization for teaching the musical arts can be noted, other than the private studies confined to wealthy burghers and aristocracy, and the

---

[29] Grout, op. cit., p. 31.

[30] Israel Rabinovitch, Of Jewish Music: Ancient and Modern. Montreal: The Book Center, 1952, p. 15.

parochial institutions. The results of Luther's efforts in promulgating religious participation through the revision of the chorale were that music did permeate German religious, communal, and domestic life. But the prevailing low level of formal music education for the masses indicates, in general, the European pattern of class systems and professional training which was still quite common through the Classic and Romantic periods.

The history of public education in the United States, in contrast, shows a consistent pattern of concern for the needs of the masses. In music education it is worthy to note that the colonial singing-school teachers ". . . aimed rather toward a citizenry versed in music as a part of a common cultural heritage." [31]

From 1838 to 1860, with the rise of the common school movement and the philosophical influences of Pestalozzi and Naegeli, it became clear that American public education would be free of religious controls. Between 1885 and 1905, methodology was the large concern stimulating pedagogical interests in music reading and the child voice. Music was by this time established as part of public education. "Music had now to prove, not its value as an art, or as contributing to our common life, but that it was a subject which could be taught effectively by the grade teacher." [32] In the twentieth century, concurrent with America's musical growth, new knowledge arose especially in psychology and philosophy which encouraged changes toward an enriched curriculum based on pragmatic principles. But the social relations of art still paralleled general developments in Europe.

With the gradual end of patronage, about 1780, and the emergence of the new middle class as a fresh agency of consumption, artistic products steadily became commodities on the open market. The dilemma of popular culture, i.e., art for the elite and art for the masses, was most apparent. During the nineteenth century, the musically bombastic effects were due in no small amount to the purse strings of this new paying public. For the philosophers, the Romantic era proved to be an aesthetic upheaval of theoretical controversy. As a result of the Industrial Revolution, the wealthy middle class, now the potential patron, desired from music an escape from reality. The strange, the remote, the imaginative, the mysterious, and the supernatural expressed their

---

[31] Charles Leonhard and Robert W. House, *Foundations and Principles of Music Education.* New York: McGraw-Hill Book Co., Inc., 1959, p. 51. Used by permission.

[32] Edward B. Birge, *History of Public School Music in the United States.* Washington: Music Educators National Conference, reprint 1966, p. 115.

predilections. The sensitive ear of the aristocratic Classicist during the Age of Reason which sought the logical clarity of form was now transformed. Goethe, as well as others, indicated the intellect of the Romanticist by claiming that art, which aimed at public entertainment or which suggested pleasant interludes of escape from chaotic living, was inferior.

> How can the public be persuaded to undertake the intellectual effort required by true art, and what can the artist do himself to facilitate the process? . . . The function of art is to facilitate productive imagination. . . . At no point must the artist stoop to the public.[33]

The popular concept of connoisseurship may also be traced to the nineteenth century. Born in the cradle of social reform, communication with and understanding of the composer was a difficult affair for the coddling masses.

> . . . they were driven to the conception of the composer as an exalted combination of priest and poet, one to whom it was given to reveal to mankind the deeper meaning of life through the divine medium of music. . . . This conception of the composer as a prophet, a heroic figure struggling against a hostile environment, also served to lend the music a quality of excitement, and emotional tension by means of which the audience was stimulated and uplifted.[34]

In America, the growing rapport between music and the masses stimulated educational interest and change, but also increased the problems of aesthetics. It was now the task of education to bridge the gap. The search for musical talent, the rise of the recording industry, new emphases on instrumental music, memory contests, and festivals — all contributed to this end.

During the first half of the twentieth century, the accomplishments of music education in extending opportunities to countless masses have been most complimentary. But the impact all this has made on mass values and tastes today is difficult to say. Can it be measured in terms of record sales, instruments purchased, or box office receipts? Have we really been educating for the goal of a musically literate and informed society? Why is music education still lagging behind other subjects which recognize changing concepts and the need for curriculum reforms?

Part of the answer lies with the deeply rooted romantic notions about music which still constitute the large bulk of instructional materials and pedagogical procedures. Music educa-

---

[33] Leo Lowenthal, *Literature, Popular Culture and Society.* Englewood Cliffs: Prentice-Hall, Inc., 1961, p. 26. Used by permission.

[34] Grout, *op. cit.,* p. 496.

tion assumed a very conservative view towards the musical and aesthetic changes of the early twentieth century.

Following World War I a number of major composers were charged with the dehumanization of art, i.e., the return to mathematical and structural foundations of art, and to doctrines of art for art's sake. Public reactions to these formalistic concerns were immediate. Opposition to trends in artistic individualism took the form of economic and political sanctions, resulting in an eclectic state of aesthetic affairs. Socialist realism, primitivism, neoromanticism, and serialism represent just a handful of the plurality of aesthetic directions on the twentieth century scene.

The aesthetic stream has questioned theories of feelings and emotions especially as these were displayed during the past romantic century. The new aesthetic is viewed by the defender as the type of art that typifies our age; hence he has not hesitated to personify beauty in the perfection of the machine and in the science of musical composition. But the absence of a well-defined, common practice adds to the difficulty in determining any one contemporary aesthetic, if only for the first half of the century. Schoenberg's duodecaphony, Stravinsky's polytonal and polyharmonic devices, Cowell's tone clusters, the microtonal music of Haba and Carillo, Varèse's percussionism, Hindemith's *Gebrauchsmusik*, Cage's indeterminancy, the tapesichord experiments of Babbit, Luening, and Ussachevsky, Stockhausen's electronic music, *musique-concrète*, and music by Illiac — all show the eclectic tendencies and individualistic styles of contemporary music.

A plurality of aesthetic directions represents the pioneering spirit of an age which seeks to test ideas and to reach out for new means in creative musical endeavors. Sound for the sake of sound and art for the sake of art have become the watchwords of the avant-garde. But considerations for the conservative consumer are inevitably implicated.

The ideal of art for everyone has degenerated to dictatorial regulation of style or the production of huge masses of cheap commercial entertainment music. Continuity of tradition has been menaced by both the passivity of its defenders and the intransigence of its attackers; Schoenberg and Webern acknowledged tradition but some of their younger disciples seem determined to annihilate the last vestiges of it. Individual freedom has been pushed to the point where composers have been alienated from the majority of potential listeners, and consequently have written music of a subjective or esoteric nature capable of being understood only by a little circle of initiates.[35]

---

[35] Grout, *op. cit.*, p. 660.

In defense, the composer states that audiences must become more involved aesthetically in the perception of new music. The composer finds it difficult to allow the low musical level of the masses to provide the standards and the criteria for his art.[36] This outlook enhances the artistic position of the expert and tends to perpetuate the concept of art for art's sake. Questions of artistic significance, of mass and individual standards, of education and of aesthetic inquiry are again at the heart of the matter.

The role played by music education in establishing aesthetic understandings in view of these musical changes has not been satisfactory. To some extent poor communication and a lack of awareness are partly to blame. But the large fault seems to lie with complacent and conservative attitudes towards artistic change in general. While changes in music education did occur, they were often motivated not by musical realizations but by educational innovations in philosophy, curriculum, and methods.

Sparked by pragmatic views, the progressive movement was launched during the second and third decades of the century. Equality of opportunity, increased concern for individual needs, abilities, and interests were expressed, among others, as desirable educational goals. Music educators embraced this liberal movement with high hopes for meaningful solutions to problems of curricula, methods, and philosophy. The mounting need to expand the narrow misconception of music education as just singing or "learning to read notes" prompted reform. The Music Educators National Conference formulated the well-known five-fold program to include listening, playing, creating, and rhythmics, as well as singing. Individuals in the profession proceeded to elaborate the suggested program into functional ideas for practice. Series books were adapted, materials were suggested; and the pattern for teacher education was modified accordingly.

More recently, the pragmatic position has been challenged by traditional forces suggesting a nostalgic return to former systems. For others, who view the contemporary problems in music, society, and cultural survival with new concern, a more radical educational position has emerged which suggests the reconstruction of culture. Within the past ten years, the position of music education in terms of general education has again been challenged. Its function and philosophy have been questioned; and its position in public school instruction stands in need of redefinition.

---

[36] Arnold Schoenberg, *Style and Idea*, New York: Philosophical Library Inc., 1950, pp. 38-39.

The philosophical issues have reached proportions of real concern. The tendency to prepare music supervisors as methodologists and as specialists, the theatrical concern over showmanship and professionally-oriented performance, the commercial enhancement of personalities in professional periodicals, the stress on the talented student, and the almost systematic disregard for musical aesthetics are all signs indicative of crisis-culture. A re-evaluation of values, and a frank appraisal of objectives appears to be vital.

Possibly the most recurrent error in the past has been the failure of instruction to remain consistent with the nature of the art. It must be evident that music is neither an intellectual pastime nor a display of technical acrobatics. . . . The true objectives of school music require a type of instruction which highlights the aesthetic experience with music itself — a methodology of breadth, patience, and inspiration.
. . . Music is *not* a specialty reserved to the "talented"; it is universally important to every human being and his culture. It can be taught frankly on that basis. . . . How much more important it is to realize that every child can be provided with all the ingredients of authentic musical experience.[37]

Considering the contemporary involvements of art and society, it is easy to understand why the traditional definition of aesthetics as philosophy of beauty is quite narrow. Emphasis has shifted from abstract considerations to more humanistic observations of artistic behavior and experience guided by applicable theoretical studies.

The progress of the musical arts within the past twenty years has been phenomenal. Never before have there been such rich resources in performance (live and recorded), in composition, in communicative media, in musicological and ethnomusicological information, and in concrete data from psychology, psychoanalysis, the social sciences, and history. The realization that the subject of aesthetics has a potential for active social influence can no longer be regarded as idle speculation, especially when one observes the potential of controlled patterns in Communist countries.[38]

Traditional Platonic views of morality and music hold that music is a reflection of a higher truth. The good was a part of the world at its inception and does not change because of customs or cultural advancements. Values are eternal and fixed, and are

---

[37] Leonhard and House, *op. cit.*, p. 65-66.
[38] See Thomas Munro, "Recent Developments in Aesthetics in America," *Journal of Aesthetics and Art Criticism,* 23 (Winter, 1964), 251-260.

misunderstood because of man's fallacious perception and understanding. In an address given in 1954, Earl E. Harper quoted Walter Goodnow Everett to the effect that "art in its nobler form is one of the quickeners of moral endeavor. This power it holds in no small degree due to the fact that it contains a transcendental element."[39] Another section of the same source book provides further support of such an "exposure" theory of music with the statements: "Beliefs are often felt rather than thought through in a rational way. Children absorb many of these ideals emotionally through direct contact with great music."[40]

Taste and appreciation according to such theory are correlative with growth in musical skill, knowledge, and the ability to comprehend and discriminate musical qualities — in short, connoisseurship.

For some, music education is rooted in empirical methods. Relevance, perception, and enjoyment must be approached from the consumer's rather than the expert's position. The role of the music teacher is to remove obstacles to perception, to remove prejudices and biases against serious music, and to help students become sensitive to the less obvious qualities of music which only training can bring into awareness. Thus music education has educational significance for everyone. If education communicates the more refined portions of musical culture to one who would not have been able to find them otherwise, then his power to control what happens to him musically and aesthetically becomes less a matter of accident.[41]

Others claim that society must insure its own survival; that education gains stature by accurately estimating its weaknesses, and by critical modification and alteration in the light of new knowledge. Those holding these viewpoints regard music education not as a special area concerned with narrow, isolated proficiencies of performance and skill, but as an aesthetic discipline which serves to color and infuse the intellectual and the scientific aspects of society. One of the important functions of music education in the secondary school, for example, would be to survey the problems of art — the meanings of art, the aesthetic

[39] Earl E. Harper, "Moral and Spiritual Values in Music Education," *Music in American Education*, Hazel N. Morgan, editor. Chicago: Music Educators National Conference, 1955, p. 8.

[40] "Music for Elementary Schools," *Music in American Education*, op. cit., p. 55.

[41] Foster MacMurray, "Pragmatism in Music Education," *Basic Concepts in Music Education*, Nelson B. Henry, editor. Chicago: University of Chicago Press, 1958, pp. 30-61.

implications, the social functions, as well as the psychological, economic, and political overtones. While these studies become more significant in higher liberal education, a meaningful introduction and application can be made in the secondary school. In this manner aesthetics aids the general student to understand the role of art, both past and present, by involvement with specific musical and social problems, and by examining the means and ends in the remaking of culture.

In the next chapter we shall explore in more detail some of these major philosophical and aesthetic theories as they bear on the practice of music education today.

CHAPTER II

THEORETICAL REVIEW

CONTEMPORARY philosophies of music bear striking resemblances to Platonic and Aristotelian themes. In the affairs of church and state, from medieval to modern concepts of the musical "good," variations in echo of Greek idealism are still evident. With the rise of humanism, the breakdown of feudalism, the growth of social libertinism, and the prevailing unprecedented crisis-culture, new heights of concern in the mass needs for aesthetic integrity have become quite apparent.

Probing articles in professional journals seek to explain the function of education in terms of aesthetic components. Critical essays analyze the means and ends in educating for musical understanding. We learn from these studies that if music is to be an integral part of contemporary life, a commitment to active involvement is essential. "Unless artists and scientists take an active part in the social struggles of our explosive age, they are opening the way to wrecking not only economic and political institutions, but the very creative freedom essential to scientific and artistic achievement."[1]

Fundamental to any intelligent course of aesthetic inquiry is an understanding of the theoretical involvements. Contemporary aesthetic theories (and sub-theories) are manifold: Croce, spiritual intuition; Maritain, moral intuition; Freud, desire and the unconscious; Santayana, reason; Langer, symbolic transformation; Garvin, feeling response; Stravinsky, speculative volition; Schoenberg, logical clarity; Leichtentritt, logical imagination; and Hindemith, symbolic craftsmanship. Certainly this listing is not inclusive, nor are the relationships mutually exclusive. But the range and depth do show the dynamic nature of aesthetic inquiry.

Furthermore, theoretical disagreements are often entangled in semantic difficulties. And of all the arts, music remains the most elusive in forms of theoretically verbalized descriptions. The student is constantly advised to "get to the music." Yet differ-

---

[1] Theodore Brameld, *Education for the Emerging Age.* New York: Harper and Bros., 1960, p. 180.

ences of opinion do exist and verbal descriptions are essential for communicative purposes at any level of instruction.

Aesthetic Theories

The basic conflict in aesthetic theory revolves about the traditional question of whether values and standards are subjective or objective, pure or emotive, specific or generic, absolute or referential. The core of disputed issues and arguments will be presented here in terms of Rader's categorization — isolationism and contextualism.[2] A third theory — relativism — will introduce a more recent theoretical position which attempts to synthesize meanings from the other two. It would be erroneous to assume, however, that these three are exclusively representative. At least two others should be noted here — complacency and eclecticism.

Characterized by lethargic outlooks which tend to discourage expressions of beliefs, the complacent attitude holds that trustworthy standards of artistic value and active commitment are not feasible. An adherence to the idea that disbelief may be wiser than positive belief may account for the obvious lack of substantial aesthetic involvement. The complacent attitude invites no philosophy of life, or of music. Musical likes and dislikes tend to become void of rational inquiry. Such primitive indifference to factors other than pure pleasure provide no answers to the riddles of musical aesthetics for either education or society.

The position which regards certain philosophic views with vague familiarity, but not in a designated commitment to action or pattern of value, is commonly known as eclecticism. While aspects of isolationism or contextualism may be appealing to the eclectic in a personal sense, a consistency of aesthetic and philosophical beliefs is missing. However, the possibilities of applying aesthetic meaning to musical situations is at least greater here than it would be at the complacent level.

An eclectic system of musical values may therefore evolve into little more than the equivalent of a musical potpourri but it can also develop into a self-asserting endeavor in which the listener tries to employ the most logical group of values to changing measure of musical worth.[3]

---

[2] Melvin Rader, editor, *A Modern Book of Esthetics*. New York: Henry Holt and Co., 1952. In this discussion the broad meanings of isolationism and contextualism are implied; that isolationism in an inclusive sense is meant to reflect the views of objectivist, purist, absolutist, formalist, etc. Similarly, contextualism points up the views of subjectivist, referentialist, expressionist, associationist, etc. The purpose of such a general approach to aesthetic theory is not to oversimplify the fine lines of differentiation, but merely to introduce the important issues.

[3] Portnoy, *The Philosopher and Music*, op. cit., p. 237.

Intermediary value-beliefs as voiced by skeptical and agnostic choices must be rejected for obvious reasons. Neither would offer solutions, and both are neutral and noncommital to either patterns of action or theoretical systems. They have little to offer in determining aesthetic values for music education. On the contrary, they tend to enhance and complicate issues, and to frustrate the ideas of well-meaning individuals.

Isolationism. The classification of music as a form of mathematical logic revealing innate laws of universal significance may be traced historically to the concept of a fundamental divine harmony, as theorized by Plato, Aristotle, and the Pythagoreans. In reaction to the over-sensuousness of the nineteenth century, numerous criticisms have arisen in support of a theory of isolationism — that music is primarily formal design; [4] that the classic distinction between emotional and intellectual musical content must be retained; [5] that music is an external tonal representation not involved with feelings or situations; [6] that music is conceived in terms of only the elements of sound and time; [7] that artistic significance is perceived through the articulation of musical forms; [8] that the supreme creative process and "mysterious source of artistic work . . . must always remain hidden from human comprehension"; [9] that the subconscious elements of musical composition have a divine origin; [10] and that the assumption which holds that all men are equal is subject to careful definition when artistic matters are concerned.[11]

For the isolationist (purist, absolutist, formalist) the meanings of music are not describable in non-musical terms. The theoretical argumentation may be summarized as follows:

---

[4] E. Hanslick, *The Beautiful in Music,* trans. by G. Cohen. New York: Liberal Arts Press, 1957. Reprinted by permission of Bobbs-Merrill Co., Inc.

[5] Paul Hindemith, *The Composer's World.* Cambridge: Harvard University Press, 1952, see chapters two and three.

[6] H. L. Helmholtz, *On the Sensations of Tone.* New York: Dover Publications, 1954, p. 250.

[7] Igor Stravinsky, *The Poetics of Music,* trans. by A. Knodel and I. Dahl. New York: Random House, 1947, p. 28.

[8] L. A. Hiller and Leonard M. Isaacson, *Experimental Music.* New York: McGraw-Hill Book Co., 1959, p. 34.

[9] Paul Hindemith, *Craft of Musical Composition,* trans. by A. Mendel, Book I. New York: Associated Music Publishers, Inc., 1942, p. 11.

[10] Schoenberg, *Style and Idea, op. cit.,* p. 96.

[11] J. Ortega y Gasset, *The Dehumanization of Art.* New York: Doubleday and Co., Inc., 1956, p. 7.

1. Descriptive adjectives are largely irrelevant to musical understandings.

2. The element of definable expression is absent in a great amount of music.

3. Musical expression may differ from one person to another, although the same music may be equally enjoyed by both.

4. There is no necessary causal relationship between musical stimuli and a given mood reaction.

5. The more experienced a listener becomes the more he negates extra-musical content for purely musical understanding and phraseology.

The isolationist seeks to develop musical criteria from the objective musical organization, which is recognizable by experts and connoisseurs as absolute. Differences in value then become differences in musical structure. Meanings are derived from the inherent musical materials of composition.

> The thrilling effect of a theme is owing not to the supposed grief of a composer, but to the extreme intervals; not to the beating of his heart, but to the beating of the drums; not to the craving of his soul, but to the chromatic progression of the music.[12]

The difficulty in explaining verbally how pure music becomes meaningful is still apparent, since evidence of musical stimulus-response is largely introspective. Studies dealing with emotive musical behavior are often deceptive and misleading. Meyer reminds us that while studied relationships between mental sets and physiological changes have been amply demonstrated, the effect of tone has not. The isolationist's position on musical expression may weaken on the force of Meyer's psychological theory of emotions, or Langer's theory of symbolic conception, but the question of the representation of feelings still remains an important issue.

Contextualism. The aesthetic theory that "music is more than mere sounds in motion . . . that it includes ideas, emotions, stories, and even philosophies of life," [13] formulates the nucleus of the contextualist point of view. Sullivan emphasizes the value of music as an expression of human experiences, in contrast to both isolated values on one hand and the preponderance of extra-musical connotations on the other. He would accept, in other

---

[12] Hanslick, *op. cit.,* pp. 80-81.

[13] J. W. N. Sullivan, "Music as Expression," *Problems in Aesthetics,* M. Weitz, editor. New York: The Macmillan Co., 1959, p. 380.

words, the uniqueness of music as a medium for artistic expression, but would reject any hint of its isolation from life's involvements. Both formalist (isolationist) and expressionist (contextualist) would agree that music must have effects, but the difference between them lies in what these effects should be. Sullivan admits that words cannot sufficiently state musical meaning yet recognizes that musical phrases can stir human elements and arouse emotions and expectations of a spiritual context.

To the contextualist music is not an isolated affair which exists for its own sake. On the contrary it exists for our sake, enriched by and giving meaning to all forms of human behavior. Education, psychology, morality, religion, economics, politics — all are crucially involved in artistic interpretation and judgment. "Society," states Mueller, "is in a constantly evolving state in which the standards of the true, the beautiful, and the just are constantly being refashioned in the context of the times." [14] Values should be socially recognized and pragmatically constructed along broad humanistic lines. Not the expert, but the mass of men should judge the worth of musical art. The extent to which contextualist theory has affected the musical arts must be observed critically.

Tolstoy's theory of art as a language of the emotions, as moralistic aesthetics, is strongly reminiscent of Plato,[15] and has been carried to political and social extremes in the Communistic principles of contemporary Soviet music. Such social and religious condemnation of society and its art has stimulated a censorship of musical innovations, a concentrated effort in contextualist theories which regards strongly the union of music and text, and a concern over applicable subject matter lest intimate contact with the masses be lost.

It is not at all surprising or novel that political authorities should exercise control or censorship over music in contemporary society. Historical accounts of the problems encountered by musicians serving royalty and political interest are readily available. The propaganda value of music during the Italian independence movement, the Bohemian struggle for liberation, the political influences in the genesis of great musical works, the French revolutionary music of Gossec, the operas of Grétry, the satirical Beggar's Opera of Gay and Pepusch which struck a blow

---

[14] John H. Mueller, The American Symphony Orchestra. Bloomington: Indiana University Press, 1951, pp. 404-405.

[15] Leo Tolstoy, What is Art?, trans. by A. Maude. New York: Oxford University Press, 1962.

against administrative corruption in English government — all offer ample evidence of the powerful intermeshing of music and politics.

More recently, the political executives of Nazi Germany exercised a veto over musical subject matter, dictated desirable musical stylistic tastes, and extended a negative authority over the culturally established works of selected major composers. Atonality and twelve-tone composition were rejected by fascist dictatorships as *Kulturbolschewismus,* and have been discarded by the Soviets as decadent. One cannot deny that political indoctrination through and within the arts continues to exert a position of importance, not only in fascist and communistic societies but in the democracies as well. Such contextualist extremes illustrate the degree to which extra-musical associations can reach peaks of cultural and aesthetic confusion.

The desire to establish more meaningful concepts of musical expression has stimulated some important investigations by the moderate contextualists. For example, subjective positions that treat great art as direct and pure sensuous pleasure are rejected by Langer. Instead, she accepts the logical and psychological functions of symbolic transformation.

Music is not self-expression, but formulation and representation of emotions, moods, mental tensions, and resolutions — a logical picture . . . not a plea for sympathy. Feelings revealed in music are essentially . . . presented directly to our understandings, that we may grasp, realize, comprehend these feelings, without pretending to have them or imputing them to someone else.[16]

Langer approaches musical meaning symbolically, refuting literal assigned connotations, programmatic ideas, and immutable values. The symbolized content needs merely insight, for herein lies the vigor of musical expression which words cannot express. Musical values and judgments are not absolute nor are they uniquely in the hands of the expert.

There are no degrees of literal truth, but artistic truth, which in all significance, expressiveness, articulateness, has degrees; therefore works of art may be good or bad, and each must be judged on our experience of its revelations. Standards are set by the expectations of people . . . we must grasp a Gestalt quite definitely before we can perceive an implicit meaning . . . and such definite grasp requires a certain familiarity.[17]

---

[16] Suzanne K. Langer, *Philosophy in a New Key.* Cambridge: Harvard University Press, 1957, p. 222.

[17] *Ibid.,* p. 263.

Meyer, too, denies the possibility of specific connotations and concurs with Langer, that on the level of symbolic or metaphorical meaning, responses by listeners of comparatively like background may be quite similar. In addition, Meyer claims that there is a causal connection between the musical materials and their organization, and the connotation evoked. The connotation which is ultimately made concrete by the listener varies with the musical organization. The central theses of Meyer's psychological study are that emotion or affect is aroused when a tendency to respond is arrested or inhibited, and that emotional behavior is largely a learned cultural phenomenon rather than a natural one.

Most musical experience is meaningful without reference to the extra musical world. Whether a piece of music arouses connotations depends to a great extent upon the disposition and training of the individual listener and upon the presence of cues, either musical or extra musical, which tend to activate connotative processes. . . . The musical materials are the necessary causes for a given connotation, but since no summation of necessary causes can ever amount to a sufficient cause, the sufficient cause of any connotation must be supplied by the listener.[18]

The results of extreme contextualist views in contemporary society can best be illustrated by Soviet socialist realism. The USSR, in its ideological pattern for social revolution, has censored musical works which were deemed dangerous to the public welfare, and has enveloped the musical profession in political dogma. How can music commit crimes of formalism and bourgeois cosmopolitanism? How does such authoritarian practice characterize the Soviet pattern of music education?

Music in the Soviet Union serves as a tool of socialization. Artistic composition represents an accurate and faithful recording of the life process under the guidance of the Communist Party and the Soviet State. Music must assist actively in the education of Bolshevik spirit, and must artistically propagate the communist concept of truth, political fidelity, and must aesthetically portray a brighter tomorrow.[19] In accord with Tolstoy (What is Art?), musical innovations and abstract tendencies which remain detached from mass understandings are condemned as examples of formalism. The reaction of the Soviet composer was voiced in Shostakovitch's public declaration of 1931 — that there can be no music without ideology.

---

[18] Meyer, Emotion and Meaning in Music, op. cit., p. 264.
[19] George S. Counts, The Challenge of Soviet Education. New York: McGraw-Hill Book Co., 1957, p. 199.

Soviet education may be analyzed from three essential characteristics — the dogma of Marx, Engels, and Lenin, the locus of political power and authority, and the broadness of scope and conception. All three interplay in a monolithic control of education, the press, periodicals, books, calendars, amusements, entertainment, the arts, as well as radio, television, and the cinema. The ultimate purpose of music education is to solidify nationalistic and political ideologies. Courses of study for the talented as well as the general student include the development of musical skills in varying degrees of performance, composition, ear-training, and artistic taste in listening. Materials for both instructional and professional purposes are regulated by the state. The Soviet critic Z. Vartanyan wrote in *Sovietskaya Kultura,* in May 1958, that the majority of Soviet musicians "turned out to resemble each other very much in their creative character." While a high quality of instruction and ample facilities are provided, creative individuality is not fostered.

The State does not need many artists, but it wants those that it has to excel. The pupils are trained not because they have within them a burning desire for creative expression in an artistic medium, but because it is believed that their talents so trained, the pupils will later serve the best interest of the State.[20]

The new theses on school reform in 1960, posed by the USSR Council of Ministers, considered the development of good artistic taste a vital part of aesthetic education. A typical experiment involving the formation of a Society of Symphonic Music Amateurs was reported by the Soviet educator Bauman. Listening sessions were planned which included the "best" specimens of Soviet and Western music. Psychological tests administered at the conclusion of the experiment showed the following.

It was evident from the pupils' replies that they all saw in general, one and the same thing — Russian natural scenery. And this shows that to a person, even one quite inexperienced in music, much is comprehensible when he comes into immediate contact with genuine and great art. . . . Every pupil who has been "solidly" inducted in the Society is therefore appreciated as a "victory" — one more person who has become inwardly richer.[21]

---

[20] United States Office of Education, *Education in the U.S.S.R.* Washington: Government Printing Office, 1957, p. 110.

[21] D. E. Bauman, "A Society for Lovers of Symphonic Music," *Soviet Education,* 3 (January, 1960), 50.

One may well ponder over the reliability of the test as well as the validity and significance of the results. Musical theorists who have analyzed the music of Soviet composers from several objective standpoints have yet to discover a musical confirmation of such aesthetic attitudes.

Socialist realism may be considered aesthetically objectionable primarily because of the attitude of such an intolerant position to personal judgments, to the questioning of social policies, and to the exercise of aesthetic inquiry — the personal desire, ability and liberty to express opinions concerning artistic significance. The social realist may also be accused of musical dogmatism — an artistic neglect of the mainstream of musical progress. Duodecaphony, serialization, and electronic techniques of musical composition are negated in the philosophy of socialist realism along with other dynamic and experimental developments.

Certainly socialist realism has not provided a "final solution" for Soviet art. The periodic changes in the tension and release of controls seem to indicate internal political weaknesses and artistic restlessness. Nor does the pattern of Soviet education provide for an examination of contrasting aesthetic values, or for the recognition of individualized artistic creativity. Music education is not conceived of in a liberal sense, but in terms of propaganda value for socio-political principles. As such, musical aesthetics tends to become diluted, falsified, and instrumentalized to serve non-artistic ends. Philosophically, it can be stated further that neither aesthetic conformity nor aesthetic uniformity can be considered adequate substitutes for Socratic questioning.

Considering both isolationist and contextualist views, the range of aesthetic theory flows from pure tonal and temporal considerations on the one hand, to a severe socio-political integration of music and nebulous referential involvements on the other. The two have been in classic conflict, often with confused issues and extensive overgeneralizations.[22]

Isolationism tends to make art irresponsible, precious, and dehumanized. Contextualism tends to make art impure, didactic, and tendentious. If we follow the isolationist, we are in danger of falling into a sterile purism; if we follow the contextualist we are in danger of sacrificing the autonomy of art. We must therefore, retain the genuine insights of isolationist aesthetics and yet advance to the broader and richer interpretation of contextualism.[23]

---

[22] See Jean G. Harrell, "Issues in Music Aesthetics," *Journal of Aesthetics and Art Criticism,* 23 (Winter, 1964), 197-206.

[23] Rader, *op. cit.,* p. xxx.

Although the mistakes of each consist mainly of overstatements, optimism for future agreement through such an interrelationship seems feasible. Indeed, in view of our contemporary concerns for music education and the arts in society, support for a more rational position appears to be urgent. One theory which suggests a means of interrelation is relativism.

Relativism. Not to be regarded as a position situated arbitrarily in a "middle of the road" sense, relativism is rather an active, critical original position subscribed to by a small, but growing, minority group. The broad meaning of this aesthetic theory has been expounded by Heyl.

Relativism avoids the mythical absolute values of objectivism and the irresponsible preference of subjectivism thru new interpretations of both the variable object and the valuing subject and by an emphasis upon the interrelation between them in a total situation.[24]

Relativistic outlooks have been enhanced considerably by writers in disciplines other than music and aesthetics. Kluckhohn, in anthropology; Galbraith, in economics; Maritain, in ethical morality; Mueller and Mumford, in sociology; Meyer, in psychology, as well as Dewey, James, and Mannheim — all have contributed to a philosophy of culture which seeks to avoid parochialistic attitudes, and ethnocentric pitfalls. The realization that neither isolationism nor contextualism, per se, can adequately aid in the solution to contemporary problems has promoted the need for this critical theory. Following is a summary of the relativist's criticisms of both major positions.

Criticisms of isolationism:

1. Empirical evidence indicates a lack of universal opinions as stressed by isolationists.
2. The lack of precise meaning of key terms often makes it difficult to determine whether the cleavages between isolationism and relativism are actual or semantic.
3. Values are not ontologically intrinsic, nor is man limited to one specific approach to the meaning of reality.
4. The reluctance to indulge in the search for a personal aesthetic understanding is linked with the inherent belief in a nonexistent, absolute ideal.

---

[24] Bernard C. Heyl, *New Bearings in Esthetics and Art Criticism.* New Haven: Yale University Press, 1943, p. 125.

5. The instilling of absolute standards and values in others is both aesthetically and psychologically dangerous, rather than noble.

6. Art can never be impersonal; rather it is fundamentally expression that utilizes aesthetic symbols and represents human needs.

7. The value of art is directly proportionate to that which it expresses.

8. Although art and morality may be recognized as distinctly separate, with respect to the artist and society both are related indirectly and extrinsically.

9. Isolationist theory of the survival of the good must be rejected in favor of more pragmatic views which utilize social and psychological bases for values.

10. Aesthetic perception is made keener not merely by the examination of how faithfully rules of composition have been observed, but by noting how the medium creates expression in an individualistic manner.

11. Both the specific and generic poles of isolationism and contextualism must merge if mankind is to be aesthetically enriched.

12. Both puristic and referential musical meanings depend upon learning and conditioning.

13. Formal design is insufficient in itself to account for the artistic merit of musical composition.

Criticisms directed against contextualism:

1. Subjective value theories that claim final validity on the basis of sheer intuitive certainty are committing the identical error of objective theories.

2. Mere pleasurable liking does not provide for the education and cultivation of musical tastes and, as such, makes critical attitudes useless and absurd.

3. Subjective emphases which lean toward comparative responses and psychological criticisms divert attention from objective values of the musical work itself.

4. The reasons for the survival of great musical works cannot be adequately substantiated by the pragmatic values of the masses or by other theories of affectation.

5. Significant criteria for musical criticism cannot be rationally obtained from the inconsistency of contextualist theory.

6. Inevitably the values of music are perverted when extra-musical and instrumental values are sought.

7. So long as the cultural status quo remains in a conservative or reactionary position, the contemporary listener will not make the necessary intellectual effort for the comprehension of newer aesthetic musical innovations.

8. The interpretation of subjective musical introspections is a psychiatric task, unrelated to the business of musical criticism.

9. It is too much to expect music to imitate nature, to express emotions, and to interpret dramatic situations.

10. Art becomes propagandized when linked with the moral, political, philosophical, and religious purposes of society.

11. Extreme subjectivism can result in a negation of standards and in meaningless judgments.

12. Musical logic cannot be coherently divorced from formal structure, nor from the aesthetic experience.

The relativist's attitude towards musical significance necessitates not only comprehension of the meaning of value judgments and a commitment to action, but also a satisfactory theoretical basis for evaluation. The criticisms point up general dissatisfactions with the bases of both isolationist and contextualist positions on rather fundamental principles. Langer, for instance, is accused by Heyl of philosophically misguided dogmatism.

What I object to . . . is not her exposition of music as symbolism, but her claim that a different, though widely held approach toward music should be ruled out of court. Though at one moment she condemns critics for *entirely* rejecting her symbolic interpretation of music, at other moments she herself *entirely rejects* the interpretation of music as self-expression in the face of powerful testimony to the contrary.[25]

The idea that different critical attitudes may be justified on the bases of personally derived value criteria seems obvious to the relativist. He is not engaged in the philosophical pursuit of an absolute and universal value system, but in the logical recognition that values are relative to and conditioned by cultural groups and historical periods. For this reason, the social factor plays a dominant role in his value theory. The relativist accepts (a) the axiom of logical relativism, which treats solutions to the problems of musical value as dependent on personal evaluative criteria; and (b) the axiom of psychological relativism, which claims that individual opinion should not demand universal or absolute validity.

Some reasonable theory must be held which avoids the untenable extremes of objectivism and subjectivism; for neither a critical value

---

[25] *Ibid.*, p. 139.

theory which adopts ultimate standards nor one which rejects any standard whatsoever is clear . . . what is indubitably required is a relativism which comprehends no values apart from human valuations, yet which recognizes the necessity for and the existence of sound objectives of better or worse. These, however, cannot ever be absolute or fixed, for they depend upon philosophical assumptions and upon empirical criteria which vary somewhat from individual to individual, from culture to culture. But this means that an amount of wholesome elasticity and variety is as inevitable and desirable in criticism as it is in human nature.[26]

In other words, Tolstoy's indictment of the late works of Beethoven must be criticized primarily on an understanding of Tolstoy's value theory of art and life.[27] The fact that Beethoven's late works are now considered musical masterpieces, strengthens the tendency of the relativist to treat criteria as tentative rather than absolute.

The axiom of logical relativism insists, however, that principles and criteria which serve to guide artistic evaluation be made clear in view of some critical system. "Mere liking," according to Heyl, "is an insufficient condition for the activity of valuing."

On musical values, the relativist believes that:

Standards are relative since differently constituted sorts of better men naturally subscribe to different yet equally good attitudes, artistic as well as philosophical . . . in re-evaluating relativist principles the critic concludes that differing standards sincerely held by genuine experts cannot profitably be rated. And he claims that disregard for, or rejection of this axiom provides dogmatic, misguided, and misleading criticism. Significant judgments . . . can be made, however, when the criteria of the expert are compared with those of all incompetent observers . . . artistic concepts vary enormously from types which are extremely crude to those which are highly refined.[28]

The need for relevant standards and flexible standards is stressed because of diverse musical styles which must be judged by applicable theories of value. Consequently, the relativist feels that his position is more concrete and more empirical than either the absolutist or the subjectivist. While objectivism would claim a single uniform scale for all art, and subjectivism, the absence of a scale common to two or more individuals, relativism holds that varied value scales may be equally valid, provided they are theoretically and culturally relevant to intended purposes.

---

[26] Ibid., p. 154.

[27] See Igor Stravinsky, The Poetics of Music. New York: Random House, 1947, pp. 107-124.

[28] Heyl, op. cit., p. 153.

The following qualifications are suggested by Heyl as indicative of the skilled critic or hypothetical expert:

1. Sensitivity to artistic aims and qualities of the works in judgment.

2. Wide and varied experience with the particular medium.

3. Cultural sufficiency which enables understanding of the object in its proper historical, religious, social, political, and iconographic perspective.

4. Power to detect and consider egocentric tendencies of personal preferences which may reflect in critical analyses.

5. Normality, in contrast to eccentricity, which would provide for sufficient centralization of experience so that others may participate.

6. A critical and satisfactory theoretical basis of artistic values.

Such qualifications take cognizance of the fact that the changing character of musical values is commensurate with constantly evolving social fields. Artistic judgments are then also sociologically relative, since changes in culture from society to society reflect divergent interpretations of musical values.

> . . . culture presents the criteria from which men must choose, select and reject in order to lend rationale to their aspirations, their hopes and fears. Values, therefore, are relative to time and place, are culturally circumscribed and equally valid. To make any judgment as to the relative merits of any value-system we would be guilty of comparing the "incomparable" and if we did venture an opinion, would be guilty of ethnocentrism — judging others by our standards.[29]

Anthropological evidence has been influential in changing traditional concepts of the psychological perception of music. Theories that account for a universal notion of consonance and dissonance on acoustical grounds still remain untenable and objectionable. Research studies indicate that this dynamic phenomenon is a learned, culturally conditioned response relevant to psychological laws of perception, and imbedded in a negation of music as a universal language.

Gestalt psychologists have shown that understanding is not a matter of perceiving stimuli, or simple sound combinations in isolation, but is rather a matter of grouping stimuli into patterns and relating these patterns to one another. And finally, the studies of comparative

---

[29] Charles S. Clayman, "Values and the Teacher," *Journal of Education,* 143 (April, 1961), 25.

musicologists bringing to our attention the music of other cultures, have made us increasingly aware that the particular organization developed in Western music is not universal, natural, or God-given.[30]

For the relativist, musical meaning is a psychological product of expectation, an outgrowth of stylist experience and general cultural orientation. Thus the tendency for the trained musician to objectify meanings and for the untrained to subjectify becomes clear. Most important, relativism recognizes the desire for improvement, the need for the cultivation of musical taste, the reality of a plurality of values, and the need for qualitative standards.

While there is an obvious division of thought, all three theories point up the value of education as an important means of attaining worthy goals. To see how these theories are reflected in educational concepts and practices we must now center our attention on educational philosophy.

Philosophies of Education

The practical-minded music educator often shows a somewhat reluctant resistance to philosophical thoughts. Nevertheless, when personal or professional crises arise he is often confronted with the task of formulating basic concepts which reflect philosophical understandings. Complacent attitudes at such times tend to destroy any unity of purpose and invite severe criticism.

It may be the part of wisdom, therefore, for a profession to approach the searching out of its philosophy as a prudent individual approaches recommendations for surgery, namely to weigh the present and predicted ailments against the discomfort and promised relief of surgery.[31]

The need for a more meaningful philosophy of music education has been indicated by the increased complexity of state, national, and international affairs. The critical views and aspirations of music educators, in view of educational change in general, suggest that we should be doing more than what we are.

Music educators are not only responsible for teaching the skills of performance and theoretical information, but they are also responsible for the development of attitudes and value systems. While the study of aesthetics helps us to understand the nature of the musical arts and its relation to man, education

---

[30] Meyer, op. cit., p. 6.

[31] Harry S. Broudy, "Does Music Education Need a Philosophy," Music Educators Journal, 44 (November-December, 1957), 28.

should seeks ways of making aesthetic experiences occur more frequently and "at increasingly sophisticated levels of response in the lives of the young." [32]

The problem of art for art's sake in opposition to art as a means to other ends is a prime problem in aesthetics and consequently in philosophies of education. According to Morris:

> Some philosophies hold truth to be independent of men and their affairs and that men come to know it for its own sake, i.e., simply because they want to know. In contrast, other philosophies, most notably Experimentalism hold that truth always comes to be known in a circumstance of use; that is, we learn things when we need to learn them and in this sense, truth is never to be considered or sought after solely for its own sake, but always in terms of its function and use in some affair of life. [33]

Philosophy searches for consistent relationships of truth, reality, and value in a general inclusive sense. Educational philosophy may be interpreted then as applied philosophy. Our purpose now is to examine the interrelationships of aesthetic theory and music education as these pertain to four selected philosophies of education.

Idealism. The idealist believes that reality is governed by a permanent, uniform, and absolute spiritual mind. Truth is measured by correspondence with and imitation of this spiritual mind.

The aesthetic purpose in idealism is to seek the ultimate idea of the musical work. The composer's function is to romanticize and idealize the mundane thereby making the aesthetic object a pure representation of the commonplace.

> A work of art is recommended for our appreciation and for the developing appreciation of the young as they grow in taste, in the degree to which it cuts through the imperfections and blemishes of the empirical world, through the crudity and the ugliness and baseness of ordinary experience, to reveal loveliness transcendent. [34]

Musical works that qualify as true objects of cultivated taste should therefore be used in the motivation of aesthetic sensibilities. It is the prime function of the school to expose the young to that body of great music which has evoked rich aesthetic responses throughout history. Handel's *Messiah*, Beethoven's symphonies, Tchaikovsky's *Romeo and Juliet*, and Brahms' piano music would qualify.

---

[32] Van Cleve Morris, *Philosophy and the American School.* Houghton Mifflin Co., 1961, p. 235.

[33] *Ibid.*, p. 237.

[34] *Ibid.*, p. 255.

The educational task of arousing emotional responses by means of exposure is then followed by systematic studies of the subtle characteristics and symbolic implications relevant to the music, the composer, and the socio-cultural background. Foremost in promoting the development of such cultivated taste, the idealist holds to the mutual companionship of mind and feelings, for true taste and cultivated aesthetic enjoyment require exposure, objective mastery, and finally understanding.

Realism. The realist believes in a world of real existence which is independent of human opinion and desires. Rational procedures can aid us in perceiving the truth. In comparison with idealism, the realist's position is more material and less spiritual. The central artistic law is "the orderliness and rationality of nature." [35]

Music to the realist is akin to mathematics. The former's ordered and organized forms are similar to mathematical relationships; and the emotional reactions to music are comparable to those experienced in successful problem-solving. Nature possesses the essence of aesthetic goodness in its patterned order and regularity. Good music presents the rationality of nature in sound. Musical works of profound structural design, representing "what truly is not what ideally ought to be," qualify as artistic products to the realist.

A stress on the structural and formal principles of music characterizes the realist's educational position. Like the idealist, the traditional masterpieces of music assume prime importance. But pedagogically the study of musical construction comes first. Understandings of patterns in musical design and the mathematical orderliness of artistic structures are the essential ingredients of aesthetic education. In time, the symbolic, the mystic, and the emotional dimensions will also be experienced.

In contrast to idealism, the realist believes that sensuous contact with musical media in an applied manner should also be stressed. Playing an instrument is an important tactile approach for the development of mature appreciation and cultural taste.

The intrinsic enjoyment of music as an end in itself is the realist's goal. Utilitarian or functional motives detract from the value of pursuing the aesthetic experience for its own sake. The principle of use therefore, contaminates the *fineness* of music and destroys its purity. For example, the school orchestra is con-

---

[35] *Ibid.*, p. 261.

sidered more valuable for aesthetic education than the marching band, "because the latter, is at least in large measure, a means to a nonmusical end, i.e., the emotional arousal of fans at a football game." [36]

Philosophically, the idealist and realist both merge toward the aesthetic position of isolationism. Both hold to rather uniform notions of reality, truth, and value. Both value the preservation and reinforcement of the established socio-musical order in terms of its inherited structure.

Isolationism is characterized by its insistence on fixed, objective standards, on intrinsic, object-centered values, and on the need for aesthetic education which would terminate in connoisseurship. As Broudy expresses it, "The more we know about a value area, the more discriminating we become . . . connoisseurs are rarely content to return to the innocence of ignorance." [37]

Agreement on technical, formal, and expressive standards of art for the isolationist grows in relation to a maturation in expert appraisal. The task of education, therefore, is to aid the student in understanding musical works which are progressively more complex and abstract. A direct approach is formulated by Broudy, as follows:

1. Begin early and continue late to encourage creative expression in as many media as possible, so that these remain natural languages to the pupil.

2. Encourage experimentation with form to make the aesthetic attitude easy to assume and to make the pupil sensitive to form in aesthetic objects.

3. Utilize a wide variety of aesthetic activities and objects to keep in the forefront of the pupil's consciousness the endless possibilities of aesthetic creativity.

4. Introduce him gradually to more complex and subtle art products to see what aesthetic impressions he can receive.

5. Demand and insist that the pupil try aesthetic experience that requires as much intelligence, observation and discrimination as his previous achievements indicate he is capable of.[38]

Objective theories of educational values stress intellectual factors over the emotional and attitudinal, and remain conservative to direct and indirect cultural pressures. The early efforts to promote sensitivity to form culminate in habits of guided listening and attention to artistic design. Thus, form may be separated from content.

---

[36] *Ibid.*, p. 238.
[37] Broudy, *Building a Philosophy of Education, op. cit.*, p. 145.
[38] *Ibid.*, pp. 223-224.

Popular art is not studied because of the low quality of musical structure, the obvious form, the ordinary sentiment, the predictable lyrics. Whereas serious art requires serious study in formal education, popular art does not. The obviousness of AABA design in the average torch song is immediate in relation to the studied principles of sonata-allegro form. Education functions to develop the student's ability to comprehend such subtleties of structure and formal musical design.

The objective school may recognize higher and lower values, intrinsic and expressive factors, but its theoretical basis insists upon rational insights. Value standards become fixed and ultimate. By sequentially increasing the complexity and subtlety of appropriate musical experiences, proper aesthetic perception and standards of expert judgments will be developed.

Training in aesthetic perception is the cultivation of habits that discriminate details so readily that their meaning . . . is read off unconsciously and integrated in the larger but equally determinate effect that we feel as this individual expression of faith or this specifically presented case of dilapidation. Full technical aesthetic perception not only apprehends such qualitative character, but discriminates the technical and aesthetic constituents of the effect. And fully adequate aesthetic training would . . . make us so familiar with [the structural details of music] that these would all be discriminated automatically, and viewed not separately but as they have contributed to and remain integral in the presented (composition), which *feels* expert and subtle and strong.[39]

By stressing structural details, the isolationist derives standards of greater and lesser works of art — for example, the superiority of Beethoven's *Ninth Symphony* over the *Fourth*. Subtlety of musical details, abstractness of expression, and complexity of information are all characteristics of superior aesthetic examples and are therefore highly worthy as educational models.

But extreme standards of objectivity, while capable of producing commendable syntactic perception,[40] often culminate in limited and dogmatic patterns of aesthetic behavior. As a theoretical basis for contemporary music education, stress on the intellectual is noteworthy, but nevertheless questionable.

The mark of an educated person is tolerance to new ideas; and if a person well-versed in music should allow his superiority to make him intolerant to other people's values, then the purpose of his education is

[39] Prall, *Aesthetic Analysis, op. cit.*, p. 159.
[40] Abraham Moles, *Information Theory and Esthetic Perception*, trans. by Joel E. Cohen. Urbana: University of Illinois, 1966, see Chapter V.

misused. Purists in this respect, fail the democratic test; they are generally intolerant of their neighbor's musical values.[41]

It may also be argued that isolationism, as an aesthetic basis for music education, does not come to grips adequately with the problems of mass culture, of changing values, and of the plurality of values. In general, both idealists and realists subscribe to a rather conservative philosophical mission which is somewhat resistant to cultural change.[42]

For instance, Broudy states that the intellectual aspect of aesthetic education should be stressed over the attitudinal or emotional one because the latter "depends heavily on cultural pressures that are largely beyond the control of the school." He admits that social pressures may undo the accomplishments of education, but provides no adequate theory except "intellectual faith" to contend with the dilemma.

Vocation, family, friends, and the community as a whole may counteract a good deal of what the school has accomplished. Yet if the school is true to its function, it must proceed on the faith that the habits of intelligence will seek an opportunity to exercise themselves and in the long run under favorable circumstances will modify the culture so that it is less hostile to the values the school espouses.[43]

The question of whether and how it might be possible to narrow the cultural gap between school and community is not considered. What is of concern in isolationism is the aesthetic satisfaction of intellectual self-confidence, and of a striving towards connoisseurship.

The man who bases his aesthetic values of music on philosophical idealism is apt to extol the rational faculties over the sensory ones. He may overemphasize the importance of reason in aesthetic matters and minimize emotion. His values will rest on the idealist's premise that the world is divided into spirit and matter, soul and body, and that the natural laws which regulate the material body cannot govern the spiritual soul. He is likely to regard the composer and the metaphysician as co-workers who strive to unfold the "true" reality to man through music and philosophy. The metaphysician and musician will bring us closer to the ideal, the universal. They will guide us toward the spiritual realm with the aid of philosophy and permit us a fleeting glimpse of universal beauty through music.[44]

---

[41] Julius Portnoy, *Music in the Life of Man*. New York: Holt, Rinehart and Winston, 1963, p. 205.

[42] Theodore Brameld, *Philosophies of Education in Cultural Perspective*. New York: Dryden Press, 1955, p. 261.

[43] Broudy, *Building a Philosophy of Education, op. cit.*, p. 225.

[44] Portnoy, *The Philosopher and Music, op. cit.*, p. 235.

Genuine standards are possessed by the expert and can be acquired through education. Since the musical good is embodied objectively in the work of art itself, didactical exposure to certain compositions and to particular musical means is of the essence. More liberal idealists and realists agree that not simple exposure but systematic instruction will lead to desirable goals of connoisseurship. Agreement in value standards grows then in proportion with the degree of learned expertness. Broudy would include in a realist's approach to music education (a) what cannot be learned by informal means and (b) what is judged to be essential for all members of a community to know. He would exclude learning to sing popular music on the first count and disqualify learning to read an orchestral score on the second. Childish songs and primitive chants should not be taught; they are of dubious value for a peculiar few. On the other hand, Bach's chorales and Brahms' symphonies should be included, since an individual in responding to the works of Bach and Brahms "is exercising his human capacities at a higher level than is the child or savage, and to that extent he is "better" than they are, that is further along the road of self-perfection." [45]

It has been the traditional function in music education for some time to unfold musical truths, to provide value judgments, and to decide on the "proper" dosage of content and form. The fact that so little new music, experimental or otherwise, is presented in the public schools for real discrimination is an example of the conservative nature of some contemporary music educators.

While the idealist is concerned to some extent with the socio-musical fate of his students after high school, his conservativeness reminds him that the responsibility of the educator is the formal aspect of education — a first through twelfth grade affair. His desire to improve situations is often held in check by the purse strings of his particular position and by his observance of educational authority. Although the musical deficiencies of society are evident to him, the means and ends of cultural improvement remain "ivory-tower" affairs. When essential changes are effected his role is most often to follow the trend.

Nor would the conservative music educator provide for an adequate transevaluation of musical values among diverse cultures or among styles within a culture. Must all styles and forms of music be evaluated on a fixed, predetermined set of value criteria? Is it possible to escape from the "evils" of jazz via the

---

[45] Broudy, "A Realistic Philosophy of Music Education," *Basic Concepts in Music Education, op. cit.*, p. 77.

principle of "intellectual faith?" Is there not a solid educational need for the evaluation of good *and* poor jazz just as there is in more serious forms? If the music educator believes that school is life — a reflection of society — does it not follow that jazz too must enter the educational sanctuaries for cultural and aesthetic examination? Certainly the same reasoning would apply to social and religious issues, sex education (not just biological, but moral and social, as well), and politics. What conservative administrator would not prefer a seventh grade debate over ancient Sparta and Athens instead of over integration and segregation; or a music lesson on Tchaikovsky's *Nutcracker Suite* instead of Ussachevsky's *Rhapsodic Variations for Tape Recorder and Orchestra?* To what extent is the music educator himself impeding the dynamics of musical change, and indeed enhancing educational problems by his conservative adherence to a nebulous system of traditional and absolute values?

Aside from these critical questions, idealism and realism have contributed much in giving music education necessary academic standing and stability. Both philosophies at college level have been highly responsible for the so-called "content courses" in music literature, theory, and composition. In higher education the stress on applied skills may be attributed in large measure to the realist's philosophy. Finally, current criticisms of practices in public school music education strongly suggest a renewed emphasis on musical skills (performance, reading, as well as listening), a careful evaluation of marching and stage bands, a re-evaluation of music's intellectual values, and a marked concern for a liberal and practical familiarity with "great" literature.

Experimentalism. The experimentalist rejects all absolutes. His interest in the analysis and description of experience causes an indifference to metaphysical notions. Truth is that which is pragmatically tested and determined through actual experience. Values are constructed through the subjective judgments of men rather than on bases of idealization or imitation.

Aesthetic judgment is derived from the consequences of the interaction of music and percipient — an experiential affair.

. . . Aesthetic judgment must ultimately rest on what men respond to in their world . . . what they feel, what they sense in the presence of things which claim to be beautiful. Is Beethoven's *Ninth Symphony* beautiful? The answer does not lie in some transcendental realm of criticism, or in the verdict of the musicologist, or in some inherited criteria. The answer lies in how men feel when they hear it! . . . The purpose of the artist then, is not to behold ultimate reality and depict it for us in form, color, or sound. It is rather for him to have new insights, new feelings, new experiences, and to see how skillful he can become in enabling the rest of us to experience them too.[46]

Aesthetic education to the experimentalist functions under the general concept of learning through living. The task of music education — to arouse new meanings and new feelings of taste — begins in the experience of children. Accordingly, theories of mere exposure, systematic studies of composers and cultural backgrounds, mastery of structural laws, or intuitive perception will not bring aesthetic values and meanings closer to the daily affairs of men. Rather, tastes are acquired through direct student participation.

Start with his taste in clothes, or start with rock-'n'-roll, or start with automobile design. Or better still, start with the school. A project in the beautification of the classroom or the aesthetic improvement of the grounds would be a genuine living situation in which all kinds of aesthetic learnings could take place. Maybe it would be a project in making the cafeteria more pleasant, or a project in piping good music to the lunchroom, or a project in which the students are given the responsibility to select paintings for the hallways. Let the consequences of the youngsters' own choices be felt and undergone; let them, that is, take hold of their own experience at the aesthetic level to see what they can make of it.[47]

If there is little response, not much would be accomplished by intellectualizing, because musical standards and values are directly related to experiential levels and should be regarded as personally valid.

An individual may have learned that certain characteristics are conventionally esteemed in music; he may be able to converse with some correctness about classic music; he may honestly believe that these traits constitute his own standards. But if his own past experiences, what he has been most accustomed to and enjoyed most is ragtime, his active or working measure of evaluation are fixed on the ragtime level.[48]

The isolation of music in the concert hall is not conducive to a steady and learned cultivation of taste. The child's likes and dislikes must stand the criticism of the learner's everyday experience. To this end, the experimentalist (like the realist) wants the student to study a musical instrument. But his purpose for

---

[46] Morris, *op. cit.*, p. 273.

[47] *Ibid.*, p. 313.

[48] John Dewey, *Democracy and Education*. New York: The MacMillan Co., 1922, p. 274.

such participation (unlike the realist) is not just to involve sensual aspects, but to provide a direct experiential approach to understanding and acquired taste.

We have learned from the discussion at the beginning of this chapter that objective factors mark isolationism; subjective factors, contextualism.

Art is often entangled with other forms of culture and must therefore be interpreted in terms of its entanglements. . . . Contextualists insist more emphatically that art is entwined with non-art and that it has non-esthetic causes and effects, but more controversially assert that art as art — esthetic art — even in its purest form cannot be validly interpreted except in contextualist terms.[49]

Contextualism, as an aesthetic theory, is quite compatible with experimentalist philosophy. Both believe that aesthetic values are not object-centered, but subject centered; and that music does have some kind of emotional meaning suggestive of ordinary experience. Although the extent of precise relationships is somewhat difficult to ascertain, the aesthetic and practical are less dualistic. Further, liberal contextualists would maintain for the most part that art and aesthetic experiences are not luxuries, escapes from ordinary life, rigid disciplines undertaken for their own sake, nor simply interesting and unique pastimes. Education implies, therefore, more than an accumulation of knowledge about musical elements and structural rules.

Musical education may have, at a certain stage, to urge exclusiveness simply in order to direct attention to the proper place, namely, the forms of the music. But . . . the best listening . . . may be less pure, than purists like to think, and the best kind of musical experience may be one in which psychological, connotative, and imaginative elements — all kept in their due subordinate place — contribute vitally to the life of the whole.[50]

The key to music education according to experimentalism is in the enrichment of the musical experience. Aesthetic values are enhanced by means of extensively vivid relationships which point up "poetic" values in a variety of directions — musical and extramusical. The extent to which this theory has permeated the practice of music education may be observed in the five-fold program, and in corresponding educational concerns over the whole child.

Criteria for musical values may involve both expert craftsmanship and feelingful import. "Great music," according to Leonhard and House, "expresses symbolically the life of feeling

---

[49] Rader, *op. cit.*, p. xxxii.
[50] L. A. Reid, *Proceedings of the Aristotelian Society*, Vol. XLI:126, 1940-41, as quoted in Rader, *op. cit.*, p. 269.

which cannot be expressed through language or any other medium of human expression." Good music can be distinguished from "great" by applying both sensual as well as intellectual factors of melody, rhythm, harmony, and form. How the subjectivity of sensuous aspects of judgment can be properly rated is not clear. But critical responses of a purely technical nature are not sufficient, as such, to explain the significance of art: ". . . unless a feelingful response to the musical expressiveness precedes and endows the critical response, the musician or critic is divorcing himself from the art of music and furthermore, is undermining the authenticity of his criticism." [51]

While the role of emotions in music stands in need of further study, there is sufficient evidence to believe that emotional responses result from learning and conditioning. Aesthetic errors in subjective musical meanings and emotions have been indicated in Langer's analysis of symbolic expression and in Meyer's norm-deviant hypothesis. The problem of contextual music education is how to develop sensitivity not only to musical structure, but to the affective qualities of music as well. The duality of technical and emotional standards must prevail, as these are reflected in a variety of styles — both popular and serious.

Mursell developed a program of values for music education based on a five-fold approach of awareness, initiative, discrimination, insight, and skill. The aesthetic "good" in this theory is determined largely by poetic values and expressive emotional content. Contemporary music, for instance, is regarded by Mursell as a technician's art — dehumanized, because it is divorced from the poetic interpretations of human values.[52] But his experimentalist outlook soon becomes entangled with idealism. According to Mursell, "aesthetic standards are not created by personal preference . . . a composition . . . is not good because people like it. They must like it because it is good." [53] If we accept Mursell's position, then we must also be prepared to wrestle with such inconsistencies.

The difficulties of experimentalism as a desirable philosophy for aesthetic music education lie not with the emphasis on prag-

[51] Leonhard and House, *Foundations and Principles of Music Education,* *op. cit.,* p. 87. See also Leonard B. Meyer, "Some Remarks on Value and Greatness in Music," *Journal of Aesthetics and Art Criticism,* 17 (June 1959), 486-500.

[52] See the introduction to *Contemporary Music in Europe,* edited by P. H. Lang and N. Broder. New York: W. W. Norton, 1965.

[53] James L. Mursell, *Education for Musical Growth.* Boston: Ginn and Co., 1948, pp. 189-190. Used by permission.

matic behavior, nor in the reliance (in the case of more liberal positions) on double standards of form plus content, but in the manner in which expression in music is to be determined and implemented pedagogically. Undoubtedly, aesthetic communication is dependent, to some extent, on stated meanings which help to explain the significance of a particular experience or some specific musical event in terms of an emotive, feelingful response. But when such responses become heavily impregnated with rich verbalizations, with irrelevant iconographic representations, and with dubious referential associations, then musical, aesthetic, and educational validity is highly questionable.

Extreme contextualist positions which hold that emotive standards and personal preferences constitute final validity must also be questioned, since they lack a sufficient basis of reasoned musical discrimination and hence, weaken the need for aesthetic education. Indeed, the practices of music education which are under criticism today are the results of narrow emotionalisms which lack musical meaning or substance. Composer's biographies substitute for direct musical contacts; notebooks and scrapbooks, for scores; recordings and teacher-aids, for reading skills; social games and dances, for form and structure; questionable arrangements, for authentic material; the "safe" romantic standards, for the intriguing and generally unknown contemporary and medieval literature; and Broadway musical shows, for more penetrating musical repertoire.

In short, the historical and the theoretical have been bypassed in the nebulous search for "instant fun," entertainment, or pleasant musical moments. Discrimination and critical attitudes cannot possibly be held up as desirable goals, since there is too often little provision for curricular development in these directions. Perhaps the most that can be hoped for is that the child nurtures a liking for music by "exposure" to pleasant experiences. But this same liking can probably be learned without the benefit of the music supervisor's bi-monthly visit (if as often as that), or without the benefit of formal education. (Are there people who really "hate" music?) Musical discrimination is not an impossible goal. But such achievement is dependent upon and proportionate to educational involvement. Both the teacher and the student must be made aware of the fact that mature discrimination is a complex affair. The discriminative listener "works" while he listens, utilizing all musical skills and aesthetic understandings developed through formal education. His pleasure evolves from creative problem-solving — a close involvement with the interrelationships of musical ideas made meaningful by his emotional conditioning and the sum total of his theoretical knowledge. A purely sensuously-contrived curriculum, conceived on the notion that music learning and fun are entirely synonymous, may entertain students and parents, but will not educate them for discriminative musical levels.

One may criticize both contextualism and isolationism on the same grounds. Neither is duly concerned over the role of music in contemporary society; and neither contextualists or isolationists recognize, with reconstructive purpose, the potential role of the school as an agency for active social change.

Reconstructionism. Although an outgrowth of experimentalist thought, reconstructionism is unique because of its deep concern for contemporary cultural problems.

This means two things, both of them of great importance. First, in order to think clearly about philosophy and hence, about education, we must take a good, honest look at the current state of American culture to see what it requires in the way of philosophic orientation. If culture produces philosophy, then let us examine our culture first. The second grows out of the first: Every philosophy which asks for acceptance must stand the test of *cultural adequacy.* Does it, that is, satisfy the philosophic requirements of our times? [54]

The reconstructionist is opposed to idealist and realist concepts of reality based on other-worldly and predetermined systems. He would agree with the experimentalist that experience must provide the focal point for ontological beliefs, but he stresses cultural reality (i.e., determinants in terms of groups conflicts, allegiances, and conditioners) and social history as interacting forces. Truth, the active agreement about cultural means and ends, is never considered final or fixed.

Although reconstructionism is a rather new and not widely practiced approach to education, its position is gathering strength especially in theoretical, academic studies. It is because of its critical nature that this philosophy warrants careful attention in this book.

The reconstructionist believes that we are now experiencing a culture-crisis. Never before has mankind been faced with the implications of atomic disaster nor with the marvelous possibilities of space science. Not the restoration of "nostalgic patterns of truth, beauty, and reality," but critical analysis and appropriate social action will guide mankind toward desirable goals. [55]

---

[54] Morris, *op. cit.,* p. 373.

[55] Brameld, *Education for the Emerging Age, op. cit.,* p. 31.

Education becomes the logical means for mass cultural change. Galbraith in *The Affluent Society* contends that community thinking must become the educational keystone of the rising "new class" in American society. He states that schools have lost their purpose in producing critical and productive people, that the culminating affluent society has lost anthropological and economic values. Population trends show the continuous emergence of new communities, new patterns of living, and complicated intergroup relations. Other studies by social scientists, such as Riesman's *The Lonely Crowd,* reveal that man has lost his connection with the independent democratic tradition by accepting general patterns of conformity. In other words, he has lost that unique pioneer spirit which reflected the individual-mindedness of his forebears.

An aesthetic understanding of the world community would necessitate an intelligent socio-cultural and ethnomusicological study of economic, political, and religious aspects; value systems, class structures, family and leisure patterns, and historical traditions. The aesthetic functions in any society stand in direct relation to the social responsibilities of art — instruction, production, distribution, and consumption. It is unlikely, to the reconstructionist, that the inherent purposes of music in contemporary society can ever be achieved unless the professional musician and music educator accept a social integration of music. Accordingly, philosophical inquiry for the music educator would follow along these lines of inquiry:

1. How does the musician find roots in changing society without surrendering his personal aesthetic standards and values?

2. How is music education affected by social and economic change, and what aesthetic function can education perform to nurture desirable change?

3. How important are the musical arts to the community — both as art and as entertainment?

4. How could equality of opportunity operate in music education in fact, rather than in principle?

5. How are desirable changes to be determined, and how are they to be put into action? Who is to determine aesthetic needs?

6. Considering the pluralistic values of society, on what grounds can musical discrimination and artistic significance be taught?

7. Since the long tradition of private music teaching is upheld as most beneficial for the study of music, what is the real need for public school music?

8. If so many people "like music, but know little about it," does this not stand as a critical indictment of contemporary philosophy and practice in music education?

9. To what extent does the informal musical environment do more educating than the formal?

Undoubtedly, these questions suggest a redefinition of music education which would liberate its potential from the restraining confines of four walls and twelve grades, from the narrowness of specialization, and from traditional means in the preparation of the music teacher.

Reconstructionism also questions the views of critics such as Conant and Rickover, since there is little provision in their discussions for the decisive cultural role that the arts play in the present crisis. Additional electives, a longer school day, and the frantic search for the "academically" talented will not provide adequate answers to the real problems.

The reconstructionist's position on the musical arts is similar to the experimentalist's, but suggests stronger cultural purpose.

Instead of being studied "for their own sake" or for the cultivation of a "faculty" of reason, the proposed theory would have them (the arts) studied for the insight and guidance they may provide for the means and ends of education conceived in terms of cultural renascence.[56]

All subjects, including music, in Brameld's proposal are related to the hub of the curriculum — the problems and prospects of reorganizing democracy itself. The arts receive careful attention. For instance, group discussions of mass values become of import early in the secondary school.

If it is granted that today the majority of people prefer popular tunes and "soap operas" are these their deepest preferences? Or are these, rather, examples of what most people are conditioned to choose because they have been denied access to sufficient evidence of experience, and sufficient opportunities for communication of and agreement about their aesthetic wants?

If, after the evidence has been examined, consensus favors the second of these answers, what must we do in order to make symphony orchestras more numerous and available? How can books be produced more cheaply and abundantly? How can we discover, encourage, and support the artistic talent among the many who find no encouragement to develop them? [57]

---

[56] *Ibid.,* p. 36.
[57] Theodore Brameld, *Toward a Reconstructed Philosophy of Education.* Holt, Rinehart and Winston, Inc., 1956, p. 235.

Reconstructionism is utopian in essence. This vision is fundamental to its goal-seeking concern. Support comes from both ancient and modern utopianists — Plato, Augustine, Bacon, Saint-Simon, Owen; and more recently, Marx, Shaw, Mannheim, Wells, Veblen, Riesman, and Mumford. In the reconstructionist's belief, social consensus becomes the method whereby ideas are submitted for definition, appraisal, and active testing. Ample provision is made for the innovator and the unorthodox whose function it is to criticize and persuade. Truth constitutes majority agreement about goals and active means for their achievement.

Social consensus also has utopian meanings in aesthetic value-seeking.

The function of art should be to contribute to the life of man, and mankind is in the best position to judge whether its life has been actually enriched. Since the generic factor of art flows from the common life, the common man is frequently most aware of it. The masses, on the other hand, too often lack the capacity to appreciate difficult art, or to separate the specific factor, the personal and original component from its accompaniments and to judge it in itself. Perhaps there can be no reliable tribunal of esthetic judgment until mankind, split into the elite and the masses, is harmonized and made whole again.[58]

According to Maritain, "the key to our problem is a true sense of the common good and of the respect for intelligence and conscience that the common good basically requires."[59] Mumford, concerned with the lack of artistic social purpose in the advance of science and technics, suggests a merger of forces which must: ". . . lay the foundations for a united world . . . if that happens, our dreams will again become benign and open to rational discipline; our arts will recover form, structure and meaning . . ."[60]

Bacon reiterates the theme of social and economic examination of the status quo as implied in the reconstructionist's plea for open evidence and critical evaluation.

It is odd how few people realize that the nation's music is ruled from one little half a square mile of Manhattan: management, radio, recording, the union, criticism, publication, and even to some extent scholarships . . . I will not say what music young people should enjoy — but do they have the right to subject me in every public place to a jazz bath?[61]

---

[58] Rader, *op. cit.*, p. xxxvi.

[59] Jacques Maritain, *The Responsibility of the Artist*. New York: Charles Scribner's Sons, 1960, p. 85.

[60] Lewis Mumford, *Art and Technics*. New York: Columbia University Press, 1952, p. 162.

[61] Ernst Bacon, *Words on Music*. Syracuse: Syracuse University Press, 1960, pp. 5, 91.

And Barzun adds: "To sympathize with the younger composer whose quartet cannot be commercially recorded by a willing and able group of amateurs, one must be familiar with union rules, the managerial system and the recording industry." [62]

Barzun also recognizes the unprecedented nature of contemporary aesthetic problems as well as the changing role of education:

We are put for the first time in a critical position — a great advantage, which is matched and even surpassed in value by what now happens in academic teaching; with the classroom use of discs the students hears what the teacher is talking about, can test its truth by comparison and, if need be, neutralize his platitudes and prejudices by ear.[63]

Support for a social renascence of art is also affirmed by Dewey.

In an imperfect society . . . fine art will be to some extent an escape from, or an adventitious decoration of, the main activities of living. But in a better-ordered society than that in which we live, an infinitely greater happiness than is now the case would attend all modes of production. . . . In the degree in which art exercises its office, it is also a remaking of the experience of the community in the direction of greater order and unity.[64]

Meyer states the need for an aesthetic system which recognizes psychological evidence and cultural realities.

. . . new norms and their related deviants must gradually become part of the habit responses of composers, performers, and listeners alike. Such a period is usually marked by a plurality of styles. . . . the rate of change, the kind of change, and even the fact of change, all are conditioned by the social, political, and cultural climate in which the process must take place.[65]

And the need for the aesthetic infusion of music in the human endeavor is indicated by Mursell.

At the present time, many of our standards in music are thoroughly false and inimical to the best and most creative types of activity. And this is so because our art has become to some real and dangerous extent, divorced from the service and lives of men.[66]

---

[62] Jacques Barzun, *Music in American Life*. New York: Doubleday and Co., Inc., 1958, p. 27.

[63] *Ibid.*, p. 109.

[64] Dewey, *Art as Experience, op. cit.*, pp. 80-81.

[65] Meyer, *Emotion and Meaning in Music, op. cit.*, pp. 72-73.

[66] James L. Mursell, *Human Values in Music Education*. New York: Silver Burdett Inc., 1962, p. 16. Used by permission.

The aesthetic theory of relativism has an obvious appeal to the reconstructionist. Both reject absolute theories that claim fixed, eternal values, as well as theories that do not depend on sound theoretical bases. Both recognize the dependence of various approaches upon cultural and historical evidence, and upon the natural, individual, and group experience. The metaphysics of objective values and the spurious preferences of subjective interpretations are avoided by value meanings which interrelate between the object and the subject. Heyl's explanation of these qualities of relativism center about the following:

1. The potential value in a work of art becomes actual when it transacts with a sensitivity. Hence, the quality of value is somewhat dependent upon the experiencing subject.

2. Value may be considered a psychological function of animal interest, which necessitates a differentiation between valuing and mere liking. Hence, "liking is an insufficient condition for the activity of valuing." [67]

Where both isolationism and contextualism may lean toward the "desired," the "satisfying," and the "admired" good, relativism seeks the "desirable," the "satisfactory," and the "admirable." This is not to be misconceived as an idle play on words, but as an attempt to formulate a vocabulary (from a rather limited sphere) of more meaningful expression for aesthetic description.

Interpreted in this way, value theory can give meaning to our desires for improvement, to our yearnings striving for and preferring something better, and so can explain the enormous importance of training and of cultivation of taste for criticism. . . . Good and bad, better and worse are never referred to exclusively external or absolute standards but are always considered in their relation to a specific concrete subject-object situation.[68]

Relative criteria may be verified with diverse expert appaisals, but remain binding not absolutely or universally; not for the individual or the emotional moment, but for specified groups in a particular cultural and historical context. "Why should posterity always have the last word? . . . every age is entitled to its own standards of judgment in matters aesthetic." [69] Since cultural changes exercise dynamic effects upon artistic evaluations, value criteria are dependent upon the impact of relevant cultural and social developments.

---

[67] Heyl, *op. cit.*, pp. 125-126.
[68] *Ibid.*, pp. 126-127.
[69] Mueller, *op. cit.*, p. 382.

Changes in aesthetic taste and judgment . . . do not proceed from an exalted metaphysical realm . . . to the chosen few who, like the apostles of old, feel called upon to share these privileged communications with the lay masses. . . . One can only conclude that musical opinions and tastes, like political and economic preferences, are forged in a matrix of social and psychological forces and, at any given time represent a blend of traditional factors and common experiences.[70]

Such value theory may be applied to affairs other than the aesthetics of music, for example, the matter of religious preferences. What are the motivating forces which influence the individual (or the group) to accept certain principles of divine or spiritual truth? This question is often answered without much complex introspection — "I was born and raised in the particular belief," or, "There was no alternative presented to me as a child"; or, "I believe even if I do not understand all the complexities and ramifications of my particular faith"; or "I would not be comfortable in any other belief, although I admit that I understand very little of the other alternatives"; or "A steadfast faith in my beliefs prevents me from further questioning." Religious value, in this sense, is closely related to aesthetic value. To accept a religious belief or concept blindly, without the necessary personal intellectual and emotional involvement, would be contrary to relativistic theory and practice. Personal beliefs in both religion and music can gain strength and reconstructive meaning through a rational introspection of all related factors.

Viewed educationally, relativism points up the need for training as well as a renewal of faith in the democratic process of value-seeking. The principles of both relativism and reconstructionism insist upon a transevaluation of musical values, not the conservative insistence on a traditional patterned type of musical knowledge, behavior, and language.

It is not that (the) modern twelve-tone scale is necessarily beyond the ultimate comprehension of the average music lover. . . . But, without intense motivation and without belief in the infallibility of the composer, a modern audience is ill-disposed toward making the intellectual investment in an "esperanto" so long as the current language serves its aesthetic and social purpose.[71]

Does music education have a responsibility to the modern composer? To the aesthetic and artistic purposes of contemporary

---

[70] *Ibid.*, p. 384.
[71] *Ibid.*, p. 391.

society? The role of music education geared to relativistic theory is fundamentally to promote individual desire and skill in aesthetic perception. As such, it is not the educator's function to dictate likes and dislikes, nor to limit the musical "good" according to some preconceived expert knowledge, but to present a wide range of music for aesthetic analysis and criticism without prestated, teacher-imposed value judgments.

The very fact that there are many different musical style systems, both in different cultures and even within a single culture, demonstrates that styles are constructed by musicians in a particular time and place and that they are not based upon universal natural relationships inherent in the tonal material itself. And if the experience of music is not based upon natural, universal responses, it must be based upon responses which are acquired through learning.

. . . Understanding music . . . is a matter of habits acquired in one's self and properly assumed in the particular work.[72]

Valid discrimination will occur as the student becomes aware of:

1. The plurality of musical values.

2. The universal and relative dilemma.

3. The necessity for self-searching aesthetic inquiry.

4. The socio-cultural pressures which affect the meanings and values of the musical arts.

5. The psychological and cultural determinants which give rise to objective and subjective interpretations.

6. The need for a sound theoretical basis for criticism.

7. The fact that complex and subtle musical understandings require a liberal amount of theoretical and technical musical skills, and some direct experience with musical composition and creative problem-solving.

In essence, these seven points may be interpreted as a guide to education for aesthetic values. They also suggest an aesthetic framework for the musically-educated person.

Criticisms directed against relativism, as a theory which seeks to avoid the pitfalls of both isolationism and contextualism, point up weaknesses in oscillating from pole to pole and in condoning a plurality of aesthetic interpretations. For example, the belief that each kind of music is good of its kind evades the question of whether all kinds are equally good. Educationally, too, there are questions. How are disagreements to be put on an

---

[72] Meyer, *Emotion and Meaning in Music*, pp. 60-61.

empirical basis and yet resolved by "evidence?" How can the educator avoid influencing students by his own opinions and standards? Similar questions will arise about reconstructionism: Are music educators prepared both pedagogically and musically to implement such a program? Has there been sufficient preparation in the aesthetic, social, and cultural disciplines to liberate the educator from dogmatic tendencies? Are the goal-seeking ends of reconstructionist education so far removed from our traditional views that it remains impractical? To what extent will music education become "watered down" in regard to theory, literature, and performance, if our concentration is to be on socio-artistic reconstruction?

To summarize this theoretical review we conclude that:

1. A major goal of music education as derived from all theories is to raise the level of aesthetic understanding so that the complexities and subtleties of music can become more meaningful to more students through some form of systematic study.

2. No single theory of music education (nor of the aesthetic experience) is wholly adequate, comprehensive, or completely reliable for the realization of aesthetic ends.

3. Solutions to the conflict over form and content (and the consequent educational implications) cannot be found solely in the musical object, nor exclusively in the experiencing subject.

4. Each theory collects and clarifies data from diverse musical, social, and psychological sources and as such is significant as an organization of knowledge.

5. The questions that emanate from each theory about the art object are unique to the understanding of different styles of music or of different aspects within a given style.

6. One desirable outcome of music education should be the ability to modify aesthetic beliefs as warranted by sufficient evidence, both objective and subjective.

7. Each theory can be useful educationally when relevant to particular works or aesthetic problems.

8. A single eclectic formula fashioned by simply assimilating various theories could result in educational confusion.

9. Music education must function to exercise both the intellect and the emotions.

10. Because of the nature of mass education a dogmatic approach to aesthetics would be highly questionable. But the acceptance of a plurality of values by the music educator would be most consistent with our derived democratic principles.

It was the purpose of this discussion of aesthetic theories and educational philosophies to point up those ideas in theory and practice that tend to guide various approaches to music education. The implications should invite the educator to probe into further ideas and possibilities. However, a fundamental goal will have been achieved if the reader has come to realize that:

1. The aesthetic problems cannot be divorced from the problems of music education, and

2. A personal critical examination of musical and educational beliefs in relation to aesthetics is essential to the promotion of educational improvement.

In a sense, the purposes of aesthetic inquiry are largely to disturb, to urge discussion, and to suggest change where change is evidently necessary. In chapter three, we shall apply information derived thus far to some critical considerations in contemporary music education. To be consistent with the conclusions above, no attempt will be made to apply any one theory. Instead, we shall utilize what we can glean from various approaches to suggest aesthetic solutions to some "down-to-earth" problems.

CHAPTER III

CRITIQUE:

AESTHETIC VALUES IN MUSIC EDUCATION

 HILE AESTHETICS will not, in itself, solve the complicated problems of music education, its value is nevertheless most essential for meaningful solutions. The study of aesthetics helps to expose ideas and to introduce knowledge significant to the interpretation of musical and educational issues.

The perplexing questions of music education today are largely problems of aesthetic understandings. A partial list illustrating the extent to which the aesthetic dimensions have become involved would include the following:

Specialized and general music.

Intrinsic and extrinsic values.

The classroom teacher and the specialist.

The professional preparation of music teachers.

The values of the stage and marching band.

Required general music in high school.

Standards of musical literature for general music classes, for performance, and for listening.

How to teach for "appreciation."

The educational role of music in a modern curriculum of required "academic" studies.

Educational obligations toward contemporary music.

The function of music education in breeching the gap between school, society, and government.

The Problems

The concern for solutions to new and old problems and for redefinition of the educational functions of music has motivated some positive effort towards more humanistic and aesthetically-oriented concepts. For instance, there appears to be substantial agreement that the general music program should provide the core for a continuous and expanded sequence of learning from elementary through high school. According to Mursell, "general music is the trunk of a developmental program of music education . . . and the various specialties are its branches." Yet the prevailing pattern of general music education (as we have developed it) is highly inconsistent with changing socio-educational patterns. Most public school curricula include a required general music sequence from kindergarten through eighth grade. Some offer general music as an elective in the ninth grade. Few venture to include comparable studies in senior high school curricula.

All this means, that for the musically "untalented" (or academically hard-pressed at either extreme) music education terminates *formally,* in most cases, in the eighth grade. To interpret further it may be said, in effect, that the average junior high school student has received sufficient musical education by the end of the eighth grade to serve his needs as an intelligent, artistically sensitive, discriminative member of society. In any sense the varied elective offerings in choral and instrumental music from grades nine through twelve do not compensate for such an educational loss. The electives serve well as avenues of music-making (and increased learning) for those whose talents (or good fortune) allow them to participate. Such a pattern of terminative education is inconsistent with modern educational philosophy and growth in aesthetic perception.

It is no wonder that principals and general administrators regard the support of music education with reserved attitudes. Music in the schools has come to be recognized by the general educator as synonymous with entertainment, and is evaluated and consequently financed on utilitarian bases of entertainment, "background music" for school affairs, public relations, and school prestige. When confronted with problems in music education, the administrator may well inquire: "What did music education do for me, as a non-player and non-singer?" How and why were his "untalented" needs bypassed? The question presses on the conscience of music education.

The argument certainly indicates the need for a well-articulated and sequential program of musical studies from K-12 for that bulk of the school population commonly referred to as the masses. The main trunk of this program (to utilize Mursell's analogy) is synonymous with general music, while the branches (offshoots of the analogous tree) constitute the varied choral and instrumental specialties. In neglecting the trunk for the branches, the ends and means of music education have become nebulous.

The development of a pattern of general music for future consumers of the musical arts is of paramount significance in modern education. A citizenry capable of exerting artistic discrimination and value judgment would recognize the need for music education on more meaningful planes of reference. The learning sequence should make the individual cognizant — for example, through the development of listening, participation, and analytical skills — of sonata-allegro form, of design in general, of the relative merits of popular and serious music, of the creative aspects involved in "how the composer goes to work," of the social and economic forces which determine the disc-jockey's "top-ten," of electronic and tapesichord compositions, of changing historical styles, of the dissonance-consonance concept and related conditioning factors, of the problems inherent in subjective-objective evaluation, and of the significance of music as a symbolic representation of psychological stress and release manifested in terms of time and tone. These are some of the functions of a *required* general music program, both aesthetically oriented and academically sound. The need for an implementation of such a program rests with the music educator and with those professional agencies that motivate educational change. Our philosophy and curricular practices must show consistently that the masses can be educated musically.

There seems to be a real professional concern for the preservation of music as an integral study in the modern curriculum. But the business of explaining to administrators, guidance personnel, and school boards that musical studies deserve both academic and aesthetic status in general education has become more pressing. In situations where values, programs, and practices are involved, aesthetic inquiry can be helpful in clarifying issues and concepts. For example, knotty problems involving understandings of musical means and ends can be traced to the isolationist-contextualist dilemma. Whereas the goals of general education conservatively tend to stimulate contextualist ends, the sensitive teacher has often been given occasion to feel that the intrinsic values of the isolationist assume a precarious secondary level of importance. The argument requires discussion on the grounds of aesthetic education. All sides would profit from a mutual understanding of how aesthetic thought can motivate a commitment to action. Careful examination of two selected statements of educaional goals should serve to illustrate aesthetic involvement, to pinpoint the issue of intrinsic and extrinsic values, and to demonstrate the evolution of educational thought in America.

In keeping with the thinking of the times was a 1952 statement holding that:

The content of the music course should lead to good citizenship in making a pupil conscious of the spiritual and moral values which are inherent in the music which he learns. The pupil performs and hears music of various historical periods, various nations and cultures. He learns music as related to life today. Music, a language of moods and emotions, must contribute to good citizenship, if music is taught as a part of life and an expression of living itself.[1]

The Platonic overtones are evident. Just what is meant by "good citizenship" in musical meanings? Is this a rehashing of the old chestnut that "the boy who blows a horn will not blow a safe?" Are "spiritual and moral values" inherent in music, or are they culturally imposed by extra-musical factors? Is music "a language of moods and emotions," or a language at all? Do we really teach music as related to life today? The semantic difficulties in statements like this tend to mislead and to confuse the meaning and function of music education, not to mention the obvious philosophical and aesthetic entanglements. It is no wonder that the practice of music education under such a banner invited criticism from the professional musician, from the musicologist, as well as from the music educator. Can music be regarded as an academic (or artistic) study when it is justified extrinsically because of its contribution to health, citizenship, morality, and when it is conceived of as an instrument for the realization of non-musical values? Perhaps the "content of the music course" means an exposure to a selected kind or body of musical literature, since it was not too long ago that the sins of prohibition were blamed on the influence of jazz. It is significant that the statements in this same publication seven years later are of a very different nature.

Even more in contrast is the following statement which was adopted by the American Association of School Administrators in 1959:

We believe in a well-balanced school curriculum in which music, drama, painting, poetry, sculpture, architecture, and the like are included side by side with other important subjects such as mathematics, history, and science. It is important that pupils, as a part of general education, learn to appreciate, to understand, to create, and to criticize with discrimination those products of the mind, the voice, the hand, and the body which give dignity to the person and exalt the spirit of man.[2]

---

[1] "The Function of Music in the Secondary-School Curriculum," *The Bulletin of the National Association of Secondary-School Principals,* 36 (November, 1952), 8.

[2] *Your AASA in 1958-59,* Official Report. Washington, D. C.: American Association of School Administrators, 1959, pp. 248-49.

Here is a statement of functional values which could provide an aesthetic framework for the advancement of music education. "To understand, to create, to criticize" — these are the essential ingredients of aesthetic education. The "dignity" and exaltation of "the spirit of man" are humanistic concerns, reflecting both naturalistic needs for values and aspirations for loftier goals. Here, too, there is scholarly room to explore many kinds of music, to probe into the meaning and nature of the musical arts, to understand the unique function of music among the arts in general, and to develop the power to "criticize with discrimination." The resolution also emphasizes the need for music education "in a well-balanced curriculum . . . as a part of general education." As it stands, the statement signifies a potential set of beliefs for an aesthetically-oriented program.

But the question of implementation arises again. The first step towards desirable change must be the critical examination of the teacher. An aesthetic approach to music education requires a teacher who is sensitive to values and to active commitments in the search for values.

A prime example of the results of conservative neglect is the problem of music in the self-contained classroom. A 1963 questionnaire-survey made by the NEA Research Division shows the extent to which the heavy burden of musical instruction in the elementary schools has fallen on the classroom teachers. How secure are they musically? Some have completed one or two required methods courses, some have elected additional enrichment courses, while others have matriculated from colleges where music education courses are not required and in some cases not even offered. In too many states the classroom teacher is not required to have completed courses in music or music education as a prerequisite for teacher cerification. The result has been a chronic problem for the music supervisor — meeting the musical needs of classroom teachers with vastly differing backgrounds.

Music educators have reacted to this dilemma with mixed emotions. Some still rue the day when classroom teachers first assumed a musical role; some accept the situation as inevitable; while others regard the musical role of the classroom teacher as indispensable, and indeed, vital to a "modern" philosophy of education.

Although a host of applied literature has been marketed and in-service courses and workshops have been made available, no important changes in procedure and practice can be noted. Orff and Kodály-inspired pedagogy requires, in the final analysis, a musically sensitive educator. Yet the conservative and some-times complacent nature of the profession permits a "better than nothing" attitude to prevail. While publishers of texts written expressly for the classroom teacher are delighted to see sales soar (and who can blame them?), music educators, carried along by the bewildering tide, enhance and deepen the issue by frequent evidence of professional complacency. When will we be ready to admit and to defend, on both musical and educational grounds with firm philosophical convictions, that teachers prepared to teach music should be charged with this responsibility in the elmentary schools. To believe otherwise is to dilute the integrity of music education and to invite warranted criticism.

The music educator must come to question this disturbing facet of public school instruction. History and research condone the need for educational and artistic validity which is consistent with the nature of the musical arts. Musical and aesthetic sensi-tivity cannot be grasped by means of the one or two courses of-fered in the typical undergraduate preparation of the elementary teacher. An understanding of musical creativity, a liberal famili-arity with musical styles and forms, skills in making music and exploring tonal and temporal resources of Western and other cultures — these are not within the grasp of the classroom teacher who so often lacks even the basic ability to use her singing voice. Nor will the aids provided by the consultant or supervisor of music effect any long-range solution. The NEA report shows that the amount of time the average music supervisor devotes to ob-servation, demonstration, and consultation in the classroom is largely negligible. In three-fourths of the schools surveyed, the classroom teacher is solely responsible for some or all of the actual instruction.[3]

Certainly this problem calls for studied yet immediate atten-tion. The time and expense must be made available for music specialists to conduct elementary programs which are systematic and developmental in nature and which offer direct musical con-tact between the child and the specialist. In the majority of school situations economic objections are no longer applicable. To re-serve contact with the specialist for those two or three grades of general music in junior high school is to make a mockery of equality of educational opportunity and musical growth, not to mention aesthetic values.

Obviously the kind and amount of preparation of the music teacher is paramount to the implementation of any program of

---

[3] *NEA Research Bulletin*, Vol. 41, No. 2 (May 1963), pp. 56-59.

aesthetic music education. Accrediting agencies, conservatories, and schools of music must extend their preparatory programs to include not only the liberal studies of aesthetic musical theories, but also more intensive considerations of music history, musicology and ethnomusicology, and creative writing in addition to traditional practices. Courses in music education — undergraduate and graduate — could become pedagogical laboratories where aesthetic concepts in music are analyzed for active implementation in the classroom. Here, for example, the relative merits of the stage and marching band would be critically applied to value theories; standards of literature, ideas for the development of aesthetic sensitivity, and concepts and practices of aesthetic education would be developed. It should be the goal for teacher preparation, in other words, to equip the individual with both the musical skills native to his art, as well as with the aesthetic sensitivity necessary for the interpretation and practice of his profession.

Means and Ends

Educational means and ends must reflect the beliefs that musical values can be improved, that musical experiences can be aesthetically organized, and that aesthetic stimulation is a rich and necessary facet of life. The need for music education today, at all levels, stems not from the demand for more and better choirs, bands, and orchestras; not for more accomplished, professionally-bound performers (consider Barzun's analysis of the tightly-knit professional market); but rather from an unprecedented need for musical understanding. This need is the result of cultural changes which have made musical objects and interests available to the masses in a variety of directions. Concurrent with the availability of music has been the qualitative search for values, and for more meaningful understandings of the musically aesthetic experience. The music educator may well view the situation with optimism, for the function of music education is now rightfully imbedded in the desire for aesthetic understanding.

The responsibility of aesthetic education is not only the improvement of taste and discrimination, but also the development of the reasons or criteria for these. It is in the cultivation of attitudes, of experience and interaction with musical objects that music education makes it unique contribution. The problem of extending and broadening the horizons of the masses toward greater musical understanding is the basis of democratic aesthetic education.

The case for aesthetic understanding through education is strengthened further by the realization that: ". . . a casual contact with great art does not develop an art-conscious person. . . . If the music education program can have no result that would not take place in the ordinary course of events without music education, then it would have no reason for existence." [4]

Accordingly, the musically aesthetic experience cannot be conceived of as a "mystical" event in which exposure alone will produce some miraculous moment of insight, or some stimulating emotional or physiological reaction. When the compelling motive for music (listening, performing, or creating) is utilitarian, i.e., perhaps for physical or mental relaxation, one would probably achieve better results by immersing in a bathtub filled with warm water. Surely, for such purposes, as well as for mere sensuous refreshment, there is no need for formal education. All these may be included among the variety of ordinary experiences which provide for momentary delights and for emotional physical exhilarations. Values in such affairs culminate in verbalisms of likes and dislikes, similar emotionally to those mundane expressions uttered in choices of cocktails, seasoning, movie stars, Swedish massages, and the like.

Somewhat akin to religion, aesthetic involvement strives to derive meanings from ordinary experience on more abstract planes of reference to values rather than to narrowly conceived likes and dislikes. Just as sheer subjectivism as a basis for voting can be disastrous to good government, so a reliance on supposed instrumental and utilitarian values of music can be detrimental to aesthetic values. Both aesthetics and politics appeal for a greater awareness of the issues, for increased desire and right to participate, and for sufficient ability so that intelligent participation is possible. The meaning of aesthetic education is analogous to — and just as unique as — religious and political education.

Apel's definition of musical aesthetics, as stated previously, has educational merit. Music education must function to assist others in becoming critically intelligent about the relationship of musical styles and forms; about phenomena of musical time and tone; about justifications for aesthetic values; and about the humanistic import of music as an aesthetic experience. Apel's interpretation also suggests a more meaningful theoretical basis for education which would rationalize both emotive and intellectual factors.

---

[4] Leonhard and House, *Foundations and Principles of Music Education*, *op. cit.*, p. 85.

Aesthetics is a branch of knowledge; but it is knowledge of qualities in their immediacy and their immediately grasped relations, directly apprehended in sensuous structures. It is made up of generalizations of data, as all knowledge is. But its aim is intimacy with content at once sensuous and structural, readiness of grasp in this broad qualitative field. . . . Aesthetics itself is not a theory, but appreciative aesthetic experience; but it is in large part a theory of the nature of the arts, and if it tells us anything at all, it is that such knowledge requires direct acquaintance, since its total subject matter is the qualitative nature of things as presented to us directly through our sensory-affective organic functioning.[5]

Since the educator must be concerned with the aesthetic experience for which music is the stimulus, the need for tonal-temporal concentration is essential. Extra-musical ideas, iconographic references, and dramatic impulses, which "do violence to music and a disservice to the listener,"[6] must come under serious scrutiny.

The goal of intelligibility of artistic organization necessitates a stress on the stimulation of conceptual and symbolic significance, rather than on atomistic and hedonistic fragments of factual knowledge. Hence, any concentration on the formal or structural aspect of music must not be understood as an isolated acquisition of skill or information, but rather as an organic means, or intellectual tool to be utilized in applied musical understanding — i.e., in direct interaction with a musical situation. Discriminative attention to smaller musical ideas can lead through a developmental, educational process to a meaningful grasp of larger, more elaborate forms.

A man who cannot hear distinctly the difference between a major and a minor triad may learn to do so by repeatedly attending the difference between a major and a minor third. . . . In music, an elaborate variation on a theme may be mere annoying confusion for a child or for any untrained ear; but the discriminating of the constituents by analysis will teach him first to grasp them separately and then to see how they go together, and finally, all this becoming automatic, to hear the particular effect of the particular variation in its own individual character. When we know all of the arts in this way, aesthetic analysis has taught us the nature of the art.[7]

In this sense the teaching of music is comparable to the pedagogy of mathematics, and to some extent, languages and

---

[5] Prall, *Aesthetic Analysis, op. cit.*, pp. 30, 204.
[6] Schoen, "Psychological Problems in Musical Art," *op. cit.*, p. 34.
[7] Prall, *Aesthetic Analysis, op. cit.*, p. 167.

sciences. The means and ends of a well-articulated program of musical studies should be as clearly defined as they are for other academic areas. (Furthermore, since this developmental process implies growth and maturation in aesthetic analysis and judgment, the halting of required music at the junior high school level would be indicative of educational shortsightedness.)

The selection and "working-out" of musical problems are to some extent comparable to practical experiences which involve problem-solving and creative thinking. Interesting aesthetic insights can be established through analogous relationships. The normal course which musical form takes through an unfolding of musical interrelationships (thematic manipulation, cadential effect, dissonance-consonance, textural variation, and dynamic level), is closely allied with symbolic ideas in ordinary problem-solving situations. An illustration would be that we are often confronted by a number of pressing practical and personal problems. Some problems will be solved immediately; some, over a period of time. The rhythm of ordinary experience is so involved in this dynamic process that when a sufficient number of pressing problems have been eliminated, it is quite normal to seek fresh challenging experiences. As each problem runs its ordinary course, upsets may occur which stimulate selective attention and temporary solution; while at the same time, another problem may temporarily lie dormant. A distinctive characteristic of musical maturity is the "willingness to forgo immediate and perhaps lesser gratification, for the sake of future ultimate gratification." [8]

Musical creativity thrives on the abstract interpretation of this ordinary evolutionary process, serving to color and animate the practical within the uniqueness of tonal and temporal media. To develop the capacity to relate the ordinary to the aesthetic is the business of education. Most desirable for both educational and aesthetic outcomes is a liberal familiarity with the organic processes of musical composition and the musical planes of references to problem-solving techniques from simple to complex. The techniques of problem-solving and musical creativity (in its compositional sense) can be made concrete to elementary school children at various levels of understanding and experience. Probably the greatest pedagogical challenge occurs at primary and intermediate stages, where articulate and sensitive teachers are crucially needed for the task of merging the child's realm of ordinary experience with the aesthetic.

---

[8] Meyer, "Some Remarks on Value and Greatness in Music," *Journal of Aesthetics and Art Criticism*, XVII (June, 1959), 494.

Aesthetic analysis in music education is not simply a contemplative process. The performing aspect must also be considered as a vital adjunct through which aesthetic discoveries can be applied. All instrumental and vocal activities, however, should be directed to musically aesthetic ends rather than to the gymnastics of mere technical proficiency. Literature must be qualitatively selected, not for entertainment value but for aesthetic sensitiveness. The rehearsal period becomes an experience in applied understanding: where the dynamic relationship (in both ordinary and aesthetic references) can be made vivid by illustrative patterns of tonal and rhythmic stress and release, where both the formal structure and the expressive quality of music undergo analysis, and where criteria for value judgments of the "good" and the "great" are analyzed in comparative, open evidence. A library of abundantly varied musical materials reflecting diverse styles and representative historical periods is basic. Music reading skills are essential as functional means. Certainly aesthetic music education suggests the ability to utilize skills in musical performance in addition to the desire to participate.

The educator under such a plan is not a dictator of the baton, nor a "music-man" who labors under the constant pressure of demands for entertainment, but a democratic leader, whose expert status enables him to function as a moderator and guide in the aesthetic-educational process. Surely student performances are an important aspect in the socially-centered need for aesthetic communication. But performances that seek only to entertain; those that utilize musical groups as ornamental dressings, available for all occasions; and those that usurp precious rehearsal time for the preparation of pseudo-musical activities under the guise of education must be judiciously examined for aesthetic validity.

Finally, the realization of musical aesthetics in education would also necessitate a review of our more traditional means and ends. Schuman's statement of philosophy for the Juilliard School of Music suggests a more critical approach to music education and may well be applied to public school music.

It is, furthermore, our responsibility to help the student see the music of any given period in the light of its own social, political, and cultural climate; to understand that the esthetic laws and technical considerations of one period cannot be superimposed upon another; to make known to the student the varying convictions of leading musicians, both past and present, in order to help him make his own judgments; to learn that art is not concerned with conformity; to equip the student to deal with the novel without ridicule or fear of its strangeness, yet without being impressed by sheer novelty, and with the ability to probe the depth of the unfamiliar.[9]

According to this philosophy, music education assumes both democratic and musical proportions, since it would foster both musical literacy and aesthetic understanding in an atmosphere of free inquiry.

Levels of Musical Understanding

Individuals respond variously to musical stimuli, depending on their musical experience, capacity for symbolization and abstractness, cultural conditioning, and subjective likes and dislikes. To cultivate the musical tastes of others requires an understanding of the social plurality of values and how these values are shaped. The teacher must come to know not only his own system of values, but should also become aware of the systems that guide the values of his students.

A tolerant understanding is essential if education is to be effective. To limit such discussion to formal education would be naive, for the aesthetic "good" of formal education can be undone by the stimulating cultural influence of informal education.

The question once again is whether the school should merely accept the status quo, or whether it is the obligation of formal education to improve the existing socio-musical situation. If the function of music education is to be derived aesthetically, does this imply an "exposure" only to musical works deemed worthy? For the idealist, realist, the answer to the latter question would be decidedly affirmative, while the experimentalist, because of his insistence on empirical evidence, would answer negatively. To the relativist, an insistence on universal or absolute values and musical models is apt to produce most undesirable results.

A critic who attempts to instill an ideal of absolute standards and evaluations upon the unknowing and untrained may distort wholesome and just attitudes. . . . A teacher who informs pupils that one kind of art is intrinsically superior to another may be doing positive and permanent harm.[10]

The situation for the music educator may be complicated further by the particular philosophy of education in which the individual must function. Conflicting musical values, with respect to school and community, educator and educational institution,

---

[9] *The Juilliard Report on Teaching the Literature and Materials of Music.* New York: W. W. Norton and Co., Inc., 1953, p. 23. Used by permission.

[10] Heyl, *New Bearings in Esthetics and Art Criticism, op. cit.,* p. 106.

often result in a state of ambivalence and tend to promote cultural confusion.

We might approach the study of the plurality of values by noting conventional classifications of active and passive levels; or by groupings characterized by particular modes of musical responses — sensuous, associative, and syntactical.[11] However, Broudy's suggestions appear to be most appropriate for this discussion. He notes that levels of musical appreciation (understanding) fall generally into three broad categories — the emotional level, the level of general approval, and the level of discrimination.[12]

The difficulties unique to emotional levels have been indicated. Suffice it to say that the semantic problem, so directly involved in contextualist theory, is frequently the cause of confused musical understanding. To describe a succession of musical sounds in such terms as beautiful, dazzling, vigorous, pastoral, ugly, or warm exemplifies a purely sensuous approach to aesthetic perception and, consequently, calls for little if any need for formal education.

No small amount of enjoyment accrues from simply noting these aesthetic qualities — when they are pleasant. Some music is simply a succession of pleasant sounds and is enjoyed as that and nothing else. There is not much to be done here, educationally, save to expose the pupil to aesthetic objects in wide variety and to encourage him to note shapes, colors, and sounds that never would have occurred if some artist had not created them.[13]

Leonhard and House consider the emotional level on a par with fantasy-making. They too question the need for educational cultivation. Such emotional levels of musical response and understanding require little learning, "occur almost universally without guidance or organized learning," and are too often a product of factors irrelevant to the aesthetic object. To educate for pure pleasure or for sheer sensuous enjoyment there is little need for an articulated and sequential program of formal musical studies. When the goals at this level are conceived of in terms of some instrumental end — for increased leisure time, for example — then the question of aesthetic and educational function must also be appropriately weighed.

If by music for leisure one implies an oversimplification of musical and aesthetic concerns — a mere titillation of the senses

---

[11] See Meyer, "Some Remarks on Value and Greatness in Music," p. 486.
[12] Broudy, Building a Philosophy of Education, op. cit., p. 214.
[13] Ibid., pp. 215-216.

— such education is available on the open market with "built-in instructions." The interested consumer has his choice — "in ten easy lessons," "a child can play it," "surprise your wife on her birthday," "just press the green button," "let music relax you," "an album of fifty great moments in music," etc. . . . When such factors of "fun and entertainment" guide the philosophy of music education, then there is sufficient reason for regarding music in education as frivolous — as something which can be taught by simple informal exposure or by someone in a downtown music store.

Similarly, one must examine statements of philosophy (guided by the slogan "music is fun") that foster enjoyment as both a means and an end with little regard for musical or aesthetic substance. Surely music lessons in elementary schools must involve more than the fun of singing a selected number of manufactured songs accompanied by recordings (frequently highly questionable materials and presentations, at that). While it cannot be denied that true, emotional exhilarations can be worthy results of both musical intellect and feeling, the business of merely providing moments of sensuous pleasure is surely not the erudite task of the music educator. Since the level of emotional response invites little rational judgment and tends to promote pseudo-aesthetic positions of complacency and eclecticism, it would be inconsistent with a program of aesthetic education that seeks to develop standards, skills, value criteria, and some meaningful solution to the complex riddle of music's relation to man.

On the other hand, if "increased leisure time" refers to that unique socio-cultural phenomenon which points up the possibilities for the musical arts to shape, to direct, and to enrich living, there is a distinct educational function. The opportunities for increased aesthetic activity could multiply; the search for artistic significance could replace simple emotionalisms; and composers, performers, teachers, and others concerned could find new and common roots in improved interrelationships. According to this meaning, music education does have a challenging commitment.

A novel and serious challenge to Americans is posed by the remarkable increase in their leisure time. The forty-hour week and the likelihood of a shorter one, the greater life-expectancy and the earlier age of retirement, have combined to make the blessing of leisure a source of personal and community concern. "What shall I do with my spare time" all-too-quickly becomes the question "Who am I? What shall I make of my life?" When men and women find nothing within themselves but emptiness they turn to trivial and narcotic amusements, and the society of which they are a part becomes socially delinquent and potentially unstable. The humanities are the immemorial answer to man's questioning and his need for self-expression; they are uniquely equipped to fill the "abyss of leisure."

The arguments are persuasive. But, aside from the scholars themselves (who are already convinced), is anybody listening? Is anybody stirred enough to do something about "saving" the humanities before it is too late? [14]

The second level — general approval — may be characterized by a vagueness of theoretical and rational support, and by a certain reluctance to trust and to indulge in the search for personal values.

Levels of approval are usually associated with those who, in maintaining a reverence for conservativism or traditionalism, use the term " 'appreciation' in its most primitive, and passive sense, as when one 'appreciates' geometry, fair play, and democracy." [15] But all too often individual judgment becomes too vague; personal judgments, too weak. For substantiation at this level, the individual usually conforms to an established norm, or relies heavily on traditional standards and sanctions of artistic value.

Levels of general approval cut across all social classes especially in a democracy where social mobility is prevalent. The extent to which the group or environment acts as an influence on musical values may best be illustrated by the social habits of the normal teen-ager. If he wishes "to belong," he will most probably have to accept not only the social and personal mores of the group, but also its values in most matters, including music. The teen-ager who finds his musical interest in Beethoven more convincing than the current rock 'n' roll idol may also find himself ostracized from the group. To find an alternate environment of peers with whom he can identify may prove to be a difficult and possibly a psychologically disturbing move; hence, he often accepts and defends with understandable vigor the general musical standards of his acknowledged group. Comparable situations based on social needs for group conformity are also observable on adult levels. Business and common-interest groups often develop systems of similar values, at least to the extent that severe deviations from some "felt" norm might cause unfavorable singularity. Individuals at these levels place much stress on the rewards of belonging and in the comfort of conformity.

---

[14] The Commission on the Humanities, "The Plight of the Humanities," *Carnegie Review*, No. 4 (Spring, 1965), p. 21.

[15] Broudy, *Building a Philosophy of Education, op. cit.*, p. 214.

In educational areas, the social need for artistic conformity is also evident. As an illustration: The Harvard freshman may be surrounded by a "society" of lovers of Baroque music. As an upperclassman his social circle becomes more unique and more musically sophisticated. As a senior his level of general approval could conceivably center on electronic music, on Mahler, on Machaut, on Cesti, or on avant-garde jazz. At any rate, his values change with the idiosyncrasies and mobility of the particular social group. The Harvard freshman is not alone here. Levels of general approval may be observed among students at X-college or among college presidents. Revealing sociological studies have yet to be written in this field.

Aside from observing general approval levels in closed social groups, we must also note the pressures that public media of communication exert on the musical tastes of the nation. Admittedly, commercial interests support the musical fare and maintain the popular hierarchy of values. What is puzzling, however, is that the paying public accepts these as their choices.

Music "lovers" at the level of general approval frequently exhibit attitudes of complacency which ignore aesthetic inquiry. Their interests are often socially centered in some sense of belonging — i.e., the need to attend a concert, current musical comedy, or particular play because it is the thing to do, or because "everyone" is doing so. Likes and dislikes are freely voiced, but values, as such, still remain the property and business of the connoisseur or critic.

The vagueness of understandings and the narrowness of artistic concepts indicate educational deficiencies. While the level of general approval needs little formal education, a proportionate number of programs in music education can be identified here. How often have we heard these expressions from the music educator: "What can I do? My job depends on pleasing not only students, but also the principal and the parents. They *expect* to be entertained." Inadvertently, administrators and educators who indulge in giving the child what he "likes," musically, contribute to a further reluctance to seek broader aesthetic means and ends. One can justify, with some philosophical defense, Davison's appeal for a system of music education which would serve the *needs,* rather than the *wants* of man.

The third level — discrimination — calls for the important role of music education. It implies an involvement of musical skills, critical attitudes, and theoretical criteria. Primitive stages at this level may deal with elements of either rhythmic or melodic interest, but can be recognized, nevertheless, as musical, rather than purely sensuous or social.

The discriminative level is, in essence, the philosophical and aesthetic level. Here it is necessary to cope with ideas of reality, of truth, and of value. All three contemporary aesthetic theories — isolationism, contextualism, and relativism — while differing in fundamental beliefs, stress the need for greater aesthetic discrimination, abhor the dangers of baseless value judgments, and strive for the validity of their respective positions on the philosophical grounds of aesthetic inquiry.

Probably the most profound parallel to the desirability of musical discrimination may be found in the value structure of democratic society. The voter, for example, is urged to consider the issues, to know his candidate from many points of view, to weigh the party platform carefully, and finally, to exert his democratic right intelligently, by casting an individual vote. The discriminate voter demands information, engages in frequent deliberation, and cherishes his freedom to think and react independently. As further aids, not only are "facts" made public, but free transportation to the polls is often available. The key to discriminative behavior is the kind of education that allows, equips, and urges the individual to make value judgments in all matters of life — in music as well as in politics.

The increasing need for discriminative levels in music education is well supported, although, in many cases, not well defined. To illustrate, Koontz states that it is "the primary task of general music to develop the latent sensibilities of our students to beauty in all its varied forms," [16] while Krone feels that the activities of the general music class should involve many different kinds of experience so that a finer degree of discrimination will result.[17] Both suggest the need for music education to function at the level of aesthetic discrimination, but lack the refinement of practical direction and philosophical persuasiveness. If we can agree that education should function at the level of discrimination, then we must first give attention to the teacher of the masses.

Because general music classes are the only musical instruction offered to all children, the training of the teacher of these classes is far more crucial with respect to the status of music in American life, than

---

[16] James E. Koontz, "Music and General Education," *Music Educators Journal,* 42 (January, 1956), 20.

[17] Max Krone, "Jazz and the General Music Class," *Music Educators Journal,* 45 (June-July, 1959) 24.

is the training given to instrumental and choral specialists who do not come in contact with all children.[18]

To interpret this further, preparation for teaching music must include not only skills in musical proficiencies and areas of specialization, but also must promote an awareness of the desirable aesthetic level of discrimination. Certainly it would be necessary for the educator to cope with all three levels of musical understanding, both in formal and informal relationships. Individual and professional success will depend, to a large extent, on attitudes toward socio-aesthetic realities, and the willingness, desire, and skill of the teacher to transform ideas into action.

Theory and Practice

One of the notable characteristics of the musically mature individual is his ability to formulate, to maintain, and to apply standards of value judgments. The problems of values — of what makes music great, of exercising value judgments — cannot be avoided when we function at the level of discrimination. In teaching for aesthetic understanding, value is a constant educational concern.

As a teacher I decide to use this work for teaching rather than that. And though I may select the work for didactic reasons rather than because I think it is a masterpiece, even as I choose it for this reason I am aware of the distinction between a work which is great in its own terms and one which will serve to illustrate a given point clearly.[19]

Discrimination implies both a comprehension of musical value judgments and a commitment to use them. On this basis there is general agreement. Issues arise with the specific determination of value criteria. It has been noted that aesthetic conflicts invariably center about philosophical beliefs in ontology, epistemology, as well as in axiology. That is, if one accepts the metaphysical notion that all reality, truth, and value reside, inherently, in a cosmic nature, then it would normally follow that the aesthetic "good" is to be derived intrinsically — solely within the musical object. Such philosophical bases would tend, theoretically, to admit purely objective, formal, or structural artistic evidence as bases for a valid set of standards. Other theories, which may include humanistic concerns for aesthetic expression, or relative and cultural determinants, would, in all likelihood, be rejected. Since

---

[18] Melvin L. Zack, "Basic Skills for the General Music Teacher," *Music Educators Journal, 46* (September-October, 1959), 93.

[19] Meyer, "Some Remarks on Value and Greatness in Music," *op. cit.,* p. 486.

the means and ends of music education are governed to some extent by personal and theoretical beliefs, it behooves the educator to examine critically the theoretical bases, to form generalizations, and to apply derived principles in an educational setting.

There is so little general understanding of the arts in all our men of science and learning, and our masters in education itself, that all but the "authorities" in art and aesthetics on the one hand, and the virtuosi on the other, are likely to be quite unknown as forces in education, their competence or incompetence lying in a field where the ignorance of the learned leaves them free play upon the helpless younger minds for good or ill. And those who harp on standards in education are likely to be perfectly ignorant of the nature of the arts; while those critics and theorists who insist on critical standards in the arts themselves, are often consistently ignorant of the nature and function of the actual structural patterns and forms that constitute these standards.[20]

The difficulty in demonstrating the terminal validity of value criteria by external tests lies with the subjective and personal factor of aesthetic (mind-feeling) fulfillment; hence, the general difference between aesthetic and scientific opinion. (In a narrow sense, this idea has been interpreted as a discouragement for aesthetic education.) But, as Mueller suggests, "while aesthetic tastes cannot be disputed . . . their derivation may be traced and accounted for." [21]

Studies linking aesthetic value with information theory have been most interesting. While such psychological research is concerned largely with the syntactical nature of music rather than sensuous or associative, results show that logical relationships between stylistic probability systems, resistance, and musical events can be helpful, in an objective way, in determining musical value. The following summarizes Meyer's study of value and greatness in music:

1. Music that establishes no tendencies is of no value.

2. When the most probable is reached in the most immediate way, the musical event will be of little value.

3. If a goal is never reached or its active tendencies become dissipated (in elaboration or irrelevant diversion) then value will tend to be minimal.

4. As the relationships between tones are established, the probabilities of a particular goal increase.

5. Musical situations which are less predictable (low degree of probability) will contain a high degree of musical information.

[20] Prall, *Aesthetic Analysis, op. cit.,* p. 197.
[21] Mueller, *The American Symphony Orchestra, op. cit.,* p. 382.

6. Resistances or deviations disturb goal-oriented tendencies by lowering probabilities.

7. Increased information creates increased value.

8. Musical works that involve immediate satisfaction are of lesser value.

9. The "beauty" of simplicity is associative rather than structural, suggesting the security of childhood.

10. Greatness, "a quality of experience which transcends the syntactical" results in an interaction of both structural and associative elements.

Accordingly, Meyer rates Beethoven's *Ninth Symphony* as great, Debussy's *Afternoon of a Faun* as excellent, and better than Mozart's *C Major Sonata*. Similarly Bach's *Inventions* are excellent, but not great. And Schubert's songs and Chopin's preludes "can be more rewarding than some larger and more complex works" because: "information is judged not in absolute but in relative terms. For we evaluate not only the amount of information in a work but also the relation between the stimulus 'input' and the actual informational 'output'." [22]

At present, information theory in relation to musical value tends to be regarded as an esoteric study. It is generally assumed that derived meanings would be most provocative for the individual who has listened to, has studied, and has responded to a good number and variety of musical styles and desires to explore values on loftier planes of discussion. Music educators must come to examine and systematically apply such knowledge to programs, curricula, and the like.

The nurturing of opportunities for musical exploration and discovery, and for the demonstration and testing of value theories remains the responsibility of education. A fine example of such educational exploration is described in a report from the San Jose, California, Unified School District. Here, administrators, music and classroom teachers, various consultants, and a group of sixth graders collaborated in a rather ambitious undertaking — the composition of a symphony for performance by the school orchestra.

In order to solve compositional problems, it was necessary for these students to wrestle in trial and error fashion with symphonic form, major and secondary themes and their variations, melodic and rhythmic patterns, simple chords and their inversions,

---

[22] Meyer, "Some Remarks on Value and Greatness in Music," *op. cit.*, p. 497. See also Abraham Moles, *Information Theory and Esthetic Perception*, *op. cit.*, Chapter VII.

harmonic progressions, accompaniments, instrumental transpositions, and orchestration. All were outgrowths of the normal music program. The choice of instrumentation and the difficulty of music were governed by practical concerns — the instruments common to the school orchestra, and the ability level of the student performers. The total experience from conception to performance (really an accumulation of many rich learning experiences), may be regarded as a prime idea in aesthetic education involving considerations for both musical form and content.

Original expression needs encouragement, not only because it creates within the whole group, giving pleasure individually and collectively to that group, but also because it develops a deeper appreciation for all music. In this case a lasting interest in symphonic music has been fostered. The class became symphony conscious. The children began to listen in terms of their own experience. They began to look for cadences because they had tried many cadences to lend variation to their themes. They began to listen for modulation because they had felt the influence of an entirely changed mood by the simple change of key. The interweaving of melodies and countermelodies in the works of masters was more meaningful because they had learned to feel the complexity of their own problems of superimposing one melody upon another. They became increasingly respectful of the need for accuracy of details because inaccuracies in their own work led to discord and unpleasant sound.

Many of the children reached the point where they were trying to interpret the thoughts, ideas, and emotional expression underlying not only program music but also pure music. With the air so full of music, and our concert programs so complete in their offerings, it is an important outcome of the creative experience to develop appreciation for the best.[23]

Other suggestive means of realizing discriminative levels would include the development of:

1. An awareness of the basic principles of musical form and design at early stages proceeding to more involved forms in intermediate and upper grades.

2. Distinctive recognition of melody, harmony, and rhythm while music is sounding.

3. An awareness that musical discrimination often requires a recreation of the musical experience, i.e., repeated hearings.

4. A functional grasp of notation as communicative signals from composer to performer and to the listener.

---

[23] Ruth Bradley, *We Wrote a Symphony.* Evanston, Ill.: Summy-Birchard Co. 1952, pp. 3-4. Used by permission.

5. Habits of selective listening to principal and subordinate ideas which indicate the composer's purpose in the particular work.

6. Habits in concentrated (active) listening so that musical memory is strengthened and keen internal relationships are not missed. Such serious listening habits should apply to all styles of music (including jazz forms).

7. Active involvement (singing and playing) in the literature of various cultures, styles, and historical periods which exemplify both traditional and contemporary trends.

8. Revised school series books and recordings to provide units of study (not seasonal, but musical); broad introductions to Western and Eastern scale structures and rhythmic patterns as well as folk music; some basic materials for analyses of cadences, motives, phrases, formal organization; a positive approach to attitudes and skills for new music; and a liberal number of canons, part-songs, and sacred and secular music from representative eras.

9. Extensive musical exploration in intelligent, creative improvisation from the pentatonic freedom of Kodály methodology to applications in jazz improvisation.

10. Creative writing of original music at all levels, with results performed, compared, discussed, and evaluated by standards and criteria developed in class.

11. Ear training, dictation, and sight singing should not be reserved for college courses, but should belong, appropriately graded, in any systematic program of music education.

12. Habitual attention to specific musical details (imitation, ornamentation, cyclical ideas, variation, ground bass) and to musical subtleties (cadences, sound sources, timbre, tonal tendencies, modulations, harmonic nuances).

13. Critical understandings of how biographies, stories, pictures, programs, and gestures affect musical meaning and emotion.

14. Audiovisual equipment, libraries of scores and recordings, and a variety of classroom instruments, both melodic and harmonic, are basic.

15. Teachers who possess the necessary musical skills and aesthetic sensitivities to generate the setting for learning and to implement ideas into practice.

In essence, these pedagogical means are in common with those suggested by both the *Yale Seminar Report* and a recent publication of the MENC Committee on Music in General Education.[24] Both express an increasing concern for high standards, for new concepts, and for provocative action.

Educational philosophy that conceives of the school and the community as separate and isolated agencies is hostile to discriminative ends. The public view of music as entertainment can be adjusted through educational enlightenment. We must eventually come to realize that if aesthetic values imply commitments to action, then knowledge without commitment is educational irresponsibility.

Education in music, just as education in English and American literature, should strive to raise levels of taste above the comic strip or tin-pan-alley tune. Does not the status of music literature deserve the academic recognition accorded to English literature? If such recognition does not exist, then reasons should be clearly shown why and how it must and can be achieved.

What of the music educator? Will teacher education programs prepare him to deal with the complexities of aesthetic judgment and value criteria? Will he be prepared to guide himself as well as others through the cultural differentiations of various musical styles and expressions? Clayman recommends:

... that the teacher-training institution become a center for the transevaluation of cultural values, in order to extend to the teacher the opportunity to study his own values in relation to other cultures. In this way the teacher can gain invaluable insight into the "nature and nurture of man" who, strikingly diverse in his pattern of behavior, may exhibit common values.[25]

Recent developments in government subsidies and foundation support for the arts will make music available to the masses in many forms and locations. Concurrent with this encouraging and determined move is the desire for excellence and outstanding standards. In Dorian's exposition of such rising "will to culture" he indicates that the quest for quality and socio-cultural reconstruction means unprecedented possibilities for art of high quality to reach millions.[26] The idea of art for the elite and art for the masses was set back further by the establishment of a National Arts and Humanities Foundation. When President Johnson requested the creation of a National Arts Foundation in his 1965

---

[24] See Karl D. Ernst and Charles L. Gary, editors, *Music in General Education*. Washington, D. C.: Music Educators National Conference, 1965.

[25] Clayman, "Values and the Teacher," *op. cit.*, p. 26.

[26] Frederick Dorian, *Commitment to Culture: Art Patronage in Europe, Its Significance for America*. Pittsburgh: University of Pittsburgh Press, 1964.

State of the Union Message, "he was the first president since John Quincy Adams to call for federal subsidy of the arts in such a message." [27]

The general view of musical developments in America is optimistic. But while the conception of a social integration of the arts is desirable on democratic bases, we must realize the inherent problems and dangers of false standards and pseudo-aesthetic values. The unique function of music education still needs understanding. The educator must also be prepared to play a significant role in the dynamics of cultural change. Are there dangers of bureaucratic control connected with federal and state endowments? What criteria will determine the need for educational support? In what ways will Title III monies, for example, be used for aesthetic means and ends? How will the problems of aesthetic values in music education be solved by financial grants? More specifically, does not the realist's "exposure" theory support the increased availability of children's concerts? In what ways are government funds directed to the educational development of values, criteria, standards? To teacher preparation? All this is not to say that financial aid cannot be helpful, but only that careful direction and evaluation will be necessary if aesthetic results are to be realized through education.

------

[27] Robert Bernat, "Do We Really Have a Commitment to Culture?" *Carnegie Review*, 4 (Spring 1965), 12.

CHAPTER IV

RECOMMENDATIONS

*T*HE VALUE of aesthetic inquiry lies not only in the discovery of ideas but also in some form of critical application. In chapters two and three we explored the ways in which the dimensions of aesthetics permeate and give direction to the philosophy and practice of music education. In this chapter we will review and synthesize leading ideas by stating foundations, by interpreting issues, and by suggesting some avenues for research.

Foundations

I. Education provides the means whereby individual and mass musical discrimination can be realized. The development of musical skills, values, attitudes, tastes, and habits are basic to such a purpose.

II. Music education functions most effectively when both intellectual and emotional factors are considered coordinates in the development of aesthetic perception. The capacity for understanding both form and content are basic to the cultivation of musical tastes and values.

III. If aesthetic experiences contribute to a better-ordered society, then educational conditions must be fostered so that such experiences may occur more often and at more subtle levels of response. In the development of music curricula and programs, public education must center its attention on the bulk of the masses rather than on the talented few.

IV. Since no single theory of aesthetics would be universally agreeable for the needs of contemporary music education, a broad aesthetic outlook, encompassing the wealth of theories, would then be most desirable. To avoid eclecticism, which offers no factual knowledge of its own, specific theoretical understandings should be utilized when they are relevant and, hence, of value to intended purposes.

V. Music education should function within the framework of those principles of general education that outline democratic education — equal opportunity, common education, academic freedom, concensus of opinion, etc. Accordingly, educators must accept the idea of a plurality of values as basic to the pluralistic character of society and to aesthetic education. Education, as opposed to inculcation, should lead to the development of personal artistic criteria which may differ from individual to individual.

VI. The goal of raising the general level of aesthetic understanding toward more significant musical experiences requires a commitment to values which transcends mere pleasurable likes and dislikes. Educators who seek discriminative levels must be prepared to distinguish, and to guide others to distinguish, differences between mundane musical delight and artistic significance.

VII. Aesthetic music education requires an application of information from many disciplines. Such an approach enhances its academic nature and warrants its recognition in a liberal core of cultural studies, notably the humanities.

VIII. The most immediate musical needs of society are primarily consumer-oriented. To educate the masses for levels of musical understanding the guidance and connoisseurship of the expert is necessary.

IX. Music education must recognize its artistic responsibility not only to the contemporary composer, but also to the aesthetic conscience of society. Our philosophy should recognize the school as a logical agency for socio-musical change and for critical examination of aesthetic needs.

X. The aesthetic event is a connotative complex of associations made concrete by the individual. But these connotations are intracultural, not universal; conditioned, not innate; dynamic, not fixed; personal, not public.

Unlike other art forms, the musical experience may also be meaningful in a symbolic manner without reference to extramusical events. When educators rely on referential ideas foreign to music, promote unfounded notions of universal meanings, and avoid abstract symbolized meanings then the responsibility of education for aesthetic perception is neglected. While direct image-connotation and specific referential meaning is not recommended, comprehension of the materials of music is.

The listener who can thus think of music in its own terms rather than through eternal translation into something of words or mental images, is the one who most readily can approach the greatest art products in substantially the same spirit of understanding that is brought to the folk dance or popular song.[1]

---

[1] Oscar Thompson, "The Language of Music," *Perspectives on Music,* Leroy Ostransky, editor. Englewood Cliffs: Prentice-Hall Inc., 1963, p. 25.

Musical understanding results from learning, and may be approached fundamentally by grasping combinations of sounds and the successive patterns by which these sounds become interrelated. Isolated tones become meaningful when associated with other tones. Problems in the perception of rhythm, harmonic progression, texture, and formal design require similar modes of studied relationships. Habits of concentrated attention to stimulate memory and frequent comparisons to motivate critical attitudes are then essential to the task of coordinating the intellect with sense perception.

While this approach to aesthetic education would normally result in an awareness of musical factors that commonly characterize Western music, aesthetic systems of other cultures should also be introduced. Studies of intracultural variations in musical expression broaden cultural and aesthetic understandings and stimulate discriminate attitudes.

Interpretation of Issues

To implement these foundations it is important that we apply them to some practical concerns in music education. Our purpose is not only to maintain a consistency of approach from the theoretical to the practical, but also to realize meaningful aesthetic solutions to some "down to earth" issues.

Specialization and General Music. The traditional question here is whether we should direct our attention to the musically talented or to the general student. An either-or solution is inadequate, since one should not be neglected for the purpose of enhancing the other. The aesthetic foundations suggest a three-fold social concern for composer, performer, and consumer. Yet, to a considerable extent, prevailing practices in music education do show a neglect for the general music program.

It must become the responsibility of music educators to provide a program of general music through grade twelve which would result in the development of desirable levels of musical literacy and aesthetic maturity. The scope of study would evolve from these suggestions:

1. General music should provide for the development of aesthetic sensitivity through active involvement in listening, singing, instrumental playing, and creative activities. Attention to musical expression, structure, the development of skills which enhance understandings — all form the nucleus for a specific adaptation at any level.

2. General music at the secondary and collegiate levels should include, in addition, conceptual understanding of contemporary

problems of music, especially in relation to new and experimental music.

3. General music should provide for the development of discriminative habits of listening to music systematically progressing in complexity and abstractness. Judicious use may be made of programmatic ideas and iconographic representations in the lower grades. While imaginative elements may serve to motivate interests in younger people, they can prevent purposeful transitions to more abstract levels. Listening habits which are active and apperceptive foster a greater awareness of artistic significance. We must come to accept the belief that the capacity for abstract listening may be possessed by the "uneducated" listener. It remains the task of education to nurture and to develop sensitive listening levels through instruction in general music.

4. General music should provide opportunities for the study of many musical styles and aesthetic premises within relative historical and cultural contexts. The goal of musical discrimination requires a study of musical literature whose scope includes music of the pre-Baroque areas, music of Eastern cultures, of contemporary experimental music, of Soviet socialist-realism, and of so-called "popular" music — a presentation of all musical evidence for purposes of aesthetic analysis.

This interpretation of general music does not negate aspects of musical enjoyment. On the contrary, it strongly points up the consideration that meaningful enjoyment occurs with a corresponding growth in musical understanding. Education can provide for those sensuous satisfactions and musical exhilarations which are identified with the rich fulfillment of aesthetic experience.

Specialized music is an outgrowth of general music, not a substitute. Specialized activities should include not only instrumental lessons or participation in a select madrigal group, but also opportunity for extended composition, historical research, experimentation with musical acoustics, and team projects involved in community musical research and development. The goal of general music carried over into the rehearsal rooms of special performance groups create an ideal laboratory setting for more stimulating experiences and for empirical analyses. Performance, under such educational conditions, becomes a truly communicative affair based on common learnings in the social setting of performer and listener, and ideally, the composer. For these reasons, the general music program provides a democratic musical environment from which may spring the specially gifted. For these students a more intensive preparation in all aspects of music is noteworthy.

Departmentalization and Integration. The issue of departmentalization and integration has been described by Broudy as "pathological specialism." The proportions of concern extend from conflicting values within a department of music to puristic views of the autonomy of the department. Related too is the familiar question of whether music or the child is being taught.

While the music educator must be convinced of the aesthetic need for his art, his philosophical orientation must also be convincing enough so that an element of humanism permeates his relationships with others. An aesthetic approach to music education does not imply a dilution of musical integrity. On the contrary, studies will reveal that this art, in a cultural sense, cannot be understood in isolation from those social and political determinants which generate creative impulses. Hence, just as the study of Oriental musical aesthetics would normally result in a more intelligent understanding of Oriental culture, the study of Oriental culture enhances and vivifies the perception of Oriental musical aesthetics. The danger lies in pseudo-musical and cultural interpretations which are irrelevant to intended purpose.

The foundations suggest that music can be a valid source of intellectual and emotional enrichment in other study areas. But the particular music relative to such purposes must be carefully selected for its aesthetic and musical validity. Exhaustive efforts of contemporary musicologists and ethnomusicologists have resulted in a creditable array of splendid recorded materials typifying not only the historical styles of Western music but also of other cultures. These materials have been barely tapped by music educators. Rather, they tend to remain prime resource materials for the college history class, regarded by the educator as some esoteric study not applicable to the public school. Is it not possible that children can profit from this information if properly adapted and graded? Let us consider the following brief outline as an illustrative unit of study:

Unit: The History and Development of Musical Notation — Problems and Solutions.

Purpose: To study the problems of both the need to preserve music in notation and the actual evolution of written symbols of Western musical notation.

Scope: Depending on the grade level of maturity, this could extend from the ancient neumes used in the cantillations of the Hebrew *Torah* and letter notation of ancient Greece, to contemporary notational innovations in electronic and experimental music.[2]

Activities: a. Wherever feasible, discuss the relation of actual music with the visual representation. Consider different needs for preserving sound by visual means. Explore the role played by the Church. Consider the problems of notating polyphonic music and the rhythmic complexities of the Middle Ages. When and why was the bar line introduced? The clefs? The lines? How was notation affected by the development of mechanical printing?

b. Listen to representative recordings.

c. Examine illustrative examples (plates, facsimiles) from musicological sources.[3] See the four-line staff and square notations in the *Liber Usualis*.

d. Sing or play as many examples as possible from modern transcriptions.

e. Consider the problems of composers from different periods in relation to notation.

f. What notational provision is made for improvisation in Baroque music? In jazz? In aleatoric music?

g. Examine some new and experimental scores. What are the difficulties in notating and performing this music? Why have they occurred?

h. Consider the functions and problems of the musicologist. Invite one to speak to the class.

Conceptual understandings emerging from such units of study sharpen general aesthetic perception, motivate further musical study, and stimulate the development of broad cultural orientation which transcends the basic unit itself. For example, learning that "do" is not a "female deer," but a curt reminder of *dominus* (a substitution for the original *ut*), and that Guido's setting of the *Hymn to St. John* was a pedagogical solution to a problem in musical communication not only intrigues the student intellectually, but also induces a more receptive attitude towards the use of these scale syllables in the classroom. With the use of opaque or overhead projectors in coordination with recordings, Guido's hymn (in square notation and in modern transcription), the *Sumer* canon, and other delightful examples of early secular and sacred music — monophonic and polyphonic — may be

---

[2] See the scores for Stockhausen's *Studie I*, and Ussachevsky's *Rhapsodic Variations for Tape Recorder and Orchestra*.

[3] Several excellent and relatively inexpensive collections (like C. Parrish, the *Notation of the Medieval Music*, as well as W. Apel's *The Notation of Polyphonic Music*) are quite suitable for school libraries. Local colleges should have additional library resource materials.

heard, sung, and played.[4] Certainly similar units adapted to appropriate stages of understanding can be developed. With effective teaching, such important study areas can be most interesting and rewarding to public school students.

The problem of departmentalization may prevail not only from one area of the curriculum to another, but also within a single teaching area. Teachers of choral music, general music, instrumental music — band and orchestra — sometimes exercise certain aversions toward each other, just as they might be averse to "diluting" the integrity of art with other subjects in the school curriculum. The tendency to preserve the integrity of the musical arts (for one's own narrow specialty) in a multi-faceted program of education may be traced to the idealist-experimentalist conflict. Whenever objectives of general education lean towards contextualist ends, the music educator often expresses concern lest the intrinsic values of music assume a precarious secondary level of importance. Nor is the problem limited to public school music. College and university faculties often display narrow and dogmatic conceptions of specialty areas and of the relation of "pure music" to music education.

The situation can be resolved only by a common effort to agree on means and ends for aesthetic values. Specialization, as necessary as it is for all intensive purposes, must not degenerate into a diseased state of affairs. Hopefully, the time will soon arrive when composers, musicologists, performers, and educators will blend efforts in the concerted search for socio-musical improvement.

Intrinsic and Extrinsic Values. Probably the issue involving the intrinsic and extrinsic values of music requires for its resolution a deeper aesthetic insight than would be necessary for other subjects. The lack of substantial evidence about frequently stated instrumental values in terms of citizenship, leisure, therapy (mental, physiological, and criminal), and morality — all present aesthetic entanglements.

It has been emphasized that any active program of music education, sensitive to aesthetics, must delicately balance extra-musical ideas that detract from aesthetic understanding and discrimination. Simply by observation, scores of passive musical "benefits" may be noted: in restaurants, in factories, in dentist's

---

[4] Anthologies of recorded musical examples with complete and partial annotations are helpful. See *Masterpieces of Music Before 1750*, C. Parrish and J. F. Ohl, and *A Treasury of Early Music*, C. Parrish, both published by W. W. Norton and Co., Inc. in 1951 and 1958, respectively.

offices, in railroad stations; as stimulation for study, for patriotism and revolution, for worship, for relaxation, for sleep; as backgrounds to dramatic productions, to spectacles on parade, to dancing, to football games, to weddings; as song-stories of birth and death. Who can deny the social involvements of music in any of these contexts? Certainly the music educator must admit that music, in one form or another, has been utilized in an impressive variety of ways. But questions of values and educational needs still prevail.

Faith in man's capacity and ability to attain discriminate levels of musical experience provides the philosophical fuel for the educational task. Without such a fundamental belief in the means and ends of aesthetic music education, there is truly little substantial basis for mass public education in music. The sufficient role of the private music teacher, the self-taught (and successful) jazz musician, the "overnight" composer of the popular hit song, the erratic fluctuation of musical fads, and the generally complacent attitude of the public to cultural pressures, are all indicative of the fact that music will claim its own social rapport with or without formal education. The degree and qualitative extent of rapport, however, can be influenced by the educational process.

Until such time when sufficient knowledge of extra-musical values becomes available through extensive research, the educator may be doing positive harm by making unsupported extrinsic claims concerning the direct values which may be accrued from musical study and participation. Certainly there are a sufficient number of positive reasons supported on musical and aesthetic grounds which provide substantial needs for formal education. A valid program of music education will not result when music is used for purposes of emotional catharsis nor for simple satisfaction and pleasure.

A music program in the school is justified only when having a music program makes a significant difference in the student's conception of music, his understanding of it, and his competence with it. The purposes of music education are achieved only when it results in musical learning that would not take place without a music program.[5]

Curricular Development. Perceptive musical understanding can be achieved by means of a well-planned curriculum which is

---

[5] Charles Leonhard, "The Next Ten Years in Music Education," *Arizona Music News,* X (January, 1966), 9-10, 19-23, 35 and *Bulletin of Council for Research in Music Education* (Spring, 1966), 21.

both developmental and cyclical in design. Fundamental to this is the unfolding of habits of discovery and inquiry in the significance of music regardless of the particular facet of experience — performance, listening, or creativity.

1. A developmental curriculum recognizes that growth in the perception of musical stimuli requires direct and repeated interaction with these stimuli. Active participation and discussion should result in a greater perception of music's symbolic, abstract meanings.

2. The developmental process is a process of growth. Provision for appropriate levels of maturation and flexible planning commensurate with student abilities are essential.

3. A cyclical approach to program planning, cumulative in design, would be most effective. The transfer of learning from grade to grade should be achieved so that a testing of generalizations can occur with increasing maturity to less obvious forms of musical expression.

4. While exclusiveness may be necessary at certain stages to direct attention to aspects of structural form, melodic line, phrasing, and dynamics, the musical entity must always remain in the forefront. For example, for the instrumentalist or choir singer, drilling on isolated parts to achieve accuracy of performance does not, in itself, induce aesthetic thinking. The tympanist, first clarinetist, and third trumpet player in the band may read individual parts without flaws, but this accomplishment alone will not produce perceptive hearing. Superficial results can be avoided by careful attention to the musical whole. Properly utilized, discs, tape recorders, and other audiovisual aids can be most effective in creating a musical Gestalt for the boy who plays from the back row. It is necessary then for the student to understand how the specific problem relates to the generic one.

5. Creative activities for both the general and the specialized student should be fostered as natural outgrowths of the developmental process. Discovery of and experimentation with form, melody, rhythm, harmonic color, and actual musical composition are highly valid kinds of musical experiences which promote aesthetic perception.

Habits and skills in listening to and analyzing musical examples should be developed as means or tools of perception. Related activities would include various possibilities for singing, playing, and exploring tonal and temporal phenomena.

6. The developmental program reaches a significant stage in the typical college liberal arts course. A problems-approach

stressing the plurality of values, community research, and aesthetic issues in contemporary music would be most effective at this level. In addition, such a general music course would continue the development of aesthetic maturity on higher planes of abstractness utilizing live performances, visiting composers and scholars, and visits to experimental music centers both here and abroad.

7. A developmental program of aesthetic music education must provide for the rich cultivation of specialized instrumental and choral groups, as well as for careful guidance of the musically gifted. Chamber recitals by students and faculty are highly recommended. In school systems where the music staff is sufficient in number, chamber music recitals by and with teachers are a wonderful means of educational enrichment and motivation.

The inherent purpose of specialized music education is to extend the breadth and depth of musicianship beyond the practical limitations of general music. Rather than merely providing "feeder-systems" for instrumental and choral ensembles, experiences in performance and creativity for the talented student should be maintained for the purposes of enhancing aesthetic perception on higher levels of maturity. The means and ends of general music however, must permeate all specialized activities, so that all aspects of the curriculum remain consistent with common objectives.

Instrumental classes, elementary and advanced, require instruction of high calibre. Aural concepts developed through performance and demonstration are essential, especially at beginning levels. Educators who teach in the instrumental specialties must possess sufficient experience and ability in performance. It is unreasonable to assume that individuals can learn to perform adequately on all standard band and orchestral instruments during the relatively brief time allotted to teacher preparation. Where the needs arise, staff should be increased according to instrumental specialty.

While it is not the purpose here to analyze the economic implications and often nefarious outcomes of instrumental rental plans, suffice it to say that the plan by which the school owns and assigns its instrumental equipment is by far the most conducive to adequate musical growth and equality of musical opportunity. In any case, it is paramount that school instrumental teachers, as well as private teachers and music dealers who are involved with school music, understand the aesthetic means and ends which serve to guide the total program of music education.

Group experiences in instrumental and vocal activities provide excellent laboratory conditions for direct involvement with the literature of music. Rehearsals are unique opportunities for applied understanding, for new theoretical knowledge, and for extensive readings and critical evaluations of an abundance of music in varied styles. While student interests are important, the educational function demands that discriminatory levels of musical involvement be maintained. Public performance, therefore, should be the result of studies in rehearsal, reflecting values and levels of aesthetic understanding, not extra-musical events presented for purposes of pure entertainment for either students or the public.

If music educators want academic recognition, then, they must accept scholarly and educational means and ends. Entertainment, public relations, prizes, medals, and contests must be rationalized within aesthetic, educational, and academic boundaries. Algebra and trigonometry are taught with hopes of producing mathematically minded people: French and Latin, with hopes of more effective communication and understanding. None of these is taught for the prime purpose of producing a mathematician or a linguist. Music education can be approached academically and aesthetically in the same honest manner.

The purposes of choral and instrumental music are identical. Both fields of specialized musical activity have in common the study and performance of music literature. Both must seek greater aesthetic understanding through direct involvement with significant works from a broad historical repertoire. Consequently, interdepartmental friction caused by conflicting, narrow musical interests and pressures of performance can be avoided by a recognition of mutual means and ends. Each specialty bears heavily on the other in a common concern for musical growth. Both overlap in the general music class fostering a wholesome sphere of operation for the educational enterprise. Such understanding not only generates a desirable and exciting educational setting for the general as well as the musically talented student, but also provides a teaching situation conducive to aesthetic growth.

Education and Society. The foundations listed at the beginning of this chapter suggest a more inclusive role for contemporary music education, one which points to a greater concern for musical tradition, social problems, and cultural relationships.

Within the next ten years music educators must develop a music program with a higher degree of social relevance; a program that would result in the initiation and development of the musical skills and insights that would enable young people to participate in developing a worthy and meaningful musical tradition and repertory.[6]

The realization that education can be an agency for the activation of desirable musical change supports these suggestions for means and ends:

1. Music education must strive to dissipate the notion of one art for the elite and another art for the masses. The school has an important role in who shall and who shall not succeed, as well as in breaking socio-educational limitations. For these reasons it is important that the general music program functions as a required curricular hub for the total school population.

2. The school should enable the individual to participate fully in the musical life of his time — to be cognizant of cultural changes and problems, musical innovations as well as traditions. An awareness of the problems of modern music — social and aesthetic — through direct experience with recorded and live presentations is just as essential to the musically educated as is a familiarity with more traditional classics. In fact, the aesthetic disturbances often encountered in new music offer excellent aesthetic means for generating musical discovery and for discriminative experiences.

Since opportunities to hear new music are generally few, the classroom provides the ideal setting for exposure as well as analysis, active discussion, and aesthetic inquiry. Questions of what is musically "good" or "beautiful" become more critical when the student is confronted with such works as Schoenberg's *Pierrot Lunaire,* Bartók's *Sixth Quartet,* and Stockhausen's *Gesang der Juenglinge.* Mossolov's *Iron Foundry* could, for instance, motivate a study unit proceeding from Soviet socialist realism to diverse cultural entanglements of politics and music in the past.

Other trends, which reflect the eclectic innovations of twentieth-century music, include such techniques as tone-clusters, percussionism, duodecaphony and total serialization, pointalism, multirhythms and polyrhythms, bitonality and polytonality, aleatorism and indeterminism, neo-classicism and neo-romanticism, and an emerging feeling for an American music. All play a significant role in the music of our time. All must be explored in the setting of formal education.

3. The school must become more concerned with the problems of how to nurture a development of aesthetic tastes in the community. Local radio programming would be a good place to

---

[6] *Ibid.,* p. 10.

start. Why is the avid radio listener not granted a reasonable amount of musical choice when selecting across the station dial? Is the disc-jockey so religious in his personal standards? Are his choices truly indicative of mass-derived values, or are there certain economic controls which govern both public taste and broadcast music?

In the 1960's, pressing public interest in television programming caused hearings to be conducted by the Federal Communications Commission relative to the over-abundance of inferior content. Networks were concerned over the possibility of indirect, but effective, government control. The final significance of the matter, however, was not in the business of censorship as such, but in the awareness that the general public had come to press the need for distinctive programming.

Faith in such democratic endeavors should provide some initiative for music education to generate desirable changes in public channels of communication. The qualitative increase and general availability of music for public consumption can make aesthetics more meaningful to American culture; or negatively, frustrate the sincerity of aesthetic education.

Music educators must also become actively involved in research and legislation to promote desirable socio-musical changes. In other words, it is not enough to analyze the plight of the composer, performer, and educator sociologically or statistically, but active programs for improvement should be instituted.

4. Philosophical and curricular changes require satisfactory understandings among interest groups that extend beyond the teaching profession. Stress in such a rapport would be placed on the mutual realization that the value of education lies in the kind of society it produces. Not only must school parents become involved, but also diverse agencies of production and consumption. private music teachers, the American Federation of Musicians, composers' guilds, local music dealers, music publishers, composers, performers, critics, musicologists, general educators, recording corporations, clergy, school boards, civic symphony orchestras and chorales, and state and federal advisory groups which tend to influence public interest, directly or indirectly.

Publishers cannot wholly be taken to task for the dissemination of "lower-quality" music. Their prime marketing interest is regulated by sanctions of supply and demand. The materials they publish are governed, to a large extent, by the recommendations and purchases of music educators. But the printing of better music is not necessarily more expensive than that of lesser quality.

A mutual awareness of the goals of aesthetic education by music educators and publishers might make a significant difference in the musical climate.

The need for revised studies in the aesthetics of contemporary music — philosophical and applied — is also becoming increasingly important. While the principles of musical composition remain relatively unchanged, the techniques and attitudes required to perform and to listen to new music do need adaptation. Contemporary study materials and graded compositions are necessary as pedagogical aids in aesthetic perception and performance of new and experimental music.[7]

Finally, music educators' conferences must serve as professional forums for discussions of these problem areas. Certainly an increased emphasis on questions of philosophy and aesthetics at both national and regional conferences would help to clarify means and ends and stimulate educators to more active levels of interest.

Teacher Education. Since the relative success or failure of any program of music education rests ultimately with superior teaching, the type and quality of teacher preparation is of foremost interest. College preparation usually involves four broad categories — general culture, basic music, musical performance, professional education. Although general agreement in areas of curriculum and credits has been difficult to attain, national accrediting agencies have served admirably in the maintenance and improvement of standards.

Notable, however, is an increase in applied music (performance) and a decrease in professional education. Music literature, in some recent recommendations, occupies one-fourth of the forty hours allotted for general culture; professional education, twenty-four hours; basic music (ear training, harmony, counterpoint, composition, form and analysis, arranging), sixteen hours; and performance, forty hours.

It is not the intent here to propose a revised categorization, nor to suggest revisions in credit hours, although such changes may be forthcoming. Rather the prime purpose is to define the type of music educator who would most successfully meet the challenges of aesthetic education.

1. The educator's role in the development of aesthetic understanding is that of a musical and democratic expert. As such,

---

[7] Abraham A. Schwadron, "Contemporary Chamber Music for Clarinet," *The Instrumentalist*, XIX (June, 1965), pp. 73-76.

dogmatic attitudes which tend to indoctrinate must be rejected. Acceptable are the abilities (a) to translate general agreements into workable practices; (b) to distinguish between value judgments; (c) and to guide others in the formulation and testing of musical concepts which develop aesthetic understanding.

This type of educator is not only a musician, in a broad sense, but also a coordinator, a consultant, and a moderator of the aesthetic educational process, imbued with musical skill, imagination, and the ability to motivate others. Preparation for democratic leadership in musical understanding must become the keystone for the education of the teacher.

2. In addition to such attitudinal and personal qualifications, the potential music educator needs an excellent grasp of musical structure, composition, and literature. He must possess the ability to select and to demonstrate illustrative materials. He himself must be aesthetically sensitive.

While traditional preparation does provide for applied skills, too often these studies become divorced from aesthetic understanding. This kind of severe departmentalization may result in an atomistic kind of musical patchwork characterized by narrow approaches to education. The music educator needs an intelligent understanding of all periods and all styles of musical history and literature, not the fine sweep of survey courses. He must also possess functional knowledge of the theoretical and creative techniques of musical organization as applied to history and literature — including contemporary composition — not merely a saturation in the rules of common practice from Bach to Wagner. Moreover, he needs the ability to interpret such understandings aesthetically, through analysis and performance, not as knowledge or skill for the sake of technical proficiency. From this developmental core the instrumental or choral specialties should emerge with mature aesthetic perspective.

3. Studies in philosophy, aesthetics (musical and general), cultural anthropology, and the social sciences are highly recommended for inclusion in the category of general culture. The interdisciplinary effect of all becomes significant in music education courses for these purposes:

(a) To develop a broad understanding of the means and ends of music education in uplifting socio-musical values.

(b) To develop an understanding of the role of artistic conformity during periods of cultural crises.

(c) To develop professional attitudes towards the value of philosophical and aesthetic inquiry.

(d) To develop an understanding of the relative social, political, and cultural determinants as these affect the functioning of music education in a free society.

(e) To develop a liberal attitude towards creative experimentation which recognizes both the taboos of novelty and the search within the confines of the unfamiliar for new concepts of aesthetic musical expression.

(f) To develop the type of educator especially oriented to the rigors of general music, who must recognize the plurality of values, the need for aesthetic awareness, and the importance of practical, responsible action.

(g) To develop the type of educator whose aesthetic sensitivity is keen, and whose zeal for teaching is all-consuming.

(h) To develop a meaningful methodology and pedagogy to implement aesthetic theory into educational practice — not by a set of "things to do," but by stimulation of that imaginative, creative spark which marks the natural, creative teacher.

All of these call for a fresh look at both the intent and content of traditional kinds of teacher preparation. An aesthetic approach to music education requires teachers who are not only performers, enlightened by studies in history, literature, and theory, but who are also aware of those aesthetic factors that give significance to music and affect educational means and ends. A highly departmentalized preparation would detract from such purpose, and tend to restrict rather than broaden perspectives for aesthetics understanding.

Ideally, the college course in music education could serve as a hub of musical learning. Graduate studies could then be conceived on mature bases of educational and aesthetic growth emerging from actual teaching experience and culminating in further refinement of philosophy and methodology. In this way the music education class functions as a laboratory in which assimilated musical knowledge is tested and applied on educational grounds. The responsibility for planning challenging experiences, for generating stimulating discussions, and for guiding evaluations rests with the college teacher of teachers.

Heyl's qualifications for the hypothetical aesthetic expert are useful as guidelines for teacher preparation. Qualitative sensitivity, extensive experience, liberal cultural sufficiency and perspective, tolerance unmarred by egocentricity, normality over eccentricity, adequate theoretical and critical bases — all characterize the distinctive qualities of the music educator.

4. The role of the music specialist in the elementary school was discussed in chapter three. The importance of the specialist functioning in direct contact with children cannot be overstated. The practical realization of aesthetic values is, in the final analysis, a matter of providing qualified music educators.

During the next ten years music educators must establish the importance of music as a field of study by establishing a framework of specific behavioral objectives which make a difference in what the child does with and about music and a difference in the way he uses music in his life. . . . It appears obvious that a program in any subject designed to teach the basic structure of that subject requires teachers who themselves have command of the subject. . . . Well-prepared music specialists are essential in the development and the conduct of such a program.[8]

Teaching Suggestions

Aside from the teacher, the means and ends of aesthetic education are rooted in the actual experience with musical elements and critical types of related activity. The experiential approach so vital to aesthetic perception in general, has significant pedagogical value because of its potential to stimulate exploration and behavioral change. Further, a learning theory rooted in the methodology of personal discovery would be most consistent with our means and ends.

Discovery method is an exciting, stimulating, and rewarding way to learn, because the student is not provided with all the answers, but is invited to come into his own proud possession of them. . . . Adoption of discovery method would have a marked effect throughout the music education program. It could result in the development of an intrinsic, self-motivated musical interest, in the achievement of deeper aesthetic understandings, and in the growth of independence in taste and judgment.[9]

Discovery method is well suited for the development and testing of concepts, and for the cultivation of discrimination. Its reliance on research and creativity sets it apart from more traditional deductive and inductive methods. Discovery method generates the setting for learning experiences by means of leading questions, musical problems, and other resourceful challenges that invite thinking about and experience with musical ideas.

How can five tones be utilized to create feelings of tension? Can one tone be utilized to create tension? . . . What would happen if we

---

[8] Leonhard, "The Next Ten Years in Music Education," *op. cit.*, p. 10.

[9] Charles B. Fowler, "Discovery Method: Its Relevance for Music Education," *Journal of Research in Music Education*, XIV (Summer, 1966), 133-134.

took the rhythmic figurations away and just kept the melody? What would happen if we took the melody away and just kept the rhythm? What would happen if we played all the melodies on one instrument instead of the way they are scored? [10]

With appropriate adaptation by the resourceful and imaginative teacher such lines of musical inquiry could be structured in a planned grade-to-grade approach. Larger units of study (such as the unit on notation suggested previously) utilizing various relevant activities are possible. Central to the development of study areas and of the musical experiences within these areas are three ideas: (a) A methodology of discovery which stimulates the thought-provoking experience; (b) A concern for the development of both intellectual and affective concepts in aesthetic perception; (c) Student involvement in problems which are similar to but are not necessarily on the same plane as those that engage the mature, aesthetically-sensitive musician.

The final idea implies that both organization and actual presentation should lead "to a firm grasp of the nature of the discipline and to the formation and clarification of concepts basic to the discipline." In this manner, the "expert" functions as a guide in making music a study "that enables students to behave with music the way musicians behave." [11]

The suggestions which follow point up the types of leading questions and aesthetic problems which should provide concrete ideas to the music educator. With some careful thought they could be adapted and structured as actual experiences highly suitable for the classroom.

On Value Judgments [12]

1. Is it really necessary to understand music in order to enjoy it? If we understood it, would we then enjoy it any more or less?

2. What is meant by *good* music? On what standards does the average person base his musical likes and dislikes? How can we differentiate between liking and valuing?

3. Vases excavated from ancient ruins which were at one time functionally conceived are now viewed in museums as valuable works of art. Explain the implications for music.

---

[10] *Ibid.*, p. 131.

[11] Leonhard, "The Next Ten Years in Music Education," *op. cit.*, p. 9.

[12] The division here into separate areas is arbitrary, simply for the purpose of clarification and illustrative variety. Overlapping is unavoidable and indeed most desirable for a collective understanding of aesthetics.

4. How can qualitative and functional criteria be useful in judging the merits of a march? A symphony?

5. Is it the music itself that is "beautiful," or do our personal feelings about the music motivate value judgments?

6. If there exists such differentiation of opinion among connoisseurs concerning musical values, why should we rely on them? Am I not the best judge of my own preferences?

7. Examine and discuss musical reviews in newspapers and periodicals. To what extent do these really reflect musical and aesthetic understanding? What purposes are served by the critic? Assign students to write reviews of school and community concerts and analyze them in class.

8. How would mass musical preferences change if radio programmed a notable variety of musical styles?

9. The Greek Parthenon is considered both a work of art as well as an example of skillful engineering. Derive concepts and apply to musical examples such as Bach's *Passacaglia in C Minor*.

On Perceptive Listening

1. Why is it often necessary to listen more than once to a musical work in order to understand it? What does understanding music mean?

2. Is it necessary for the conductor to "entertain" audiences? In what ways do the gestures of the conductor and the performers detract from disinterested listening? Would listening become more perceptive if we could not see either the conductor or the orchestra?

3. How was it possible for Beethoven to compose while he was deaf? What is meant by the "seeing ear and hearing eye?"

4. Consider the ways in which factors of cultural conditioning can influence us during the aesthetic interaction. How do personal prejudices affect our musical values?

5. How can musical skills improve perceptive listening? Would score reading enhance or detract from the affective response? Why do musicians "analyze" music?

6. In the composition of electronic music, Stockhausen stresses the added element of space. When listening to his music close your eyes (so that the actual physical dimensions of the room are not confining) and hear some sounds "splashing" some few feet away, several rooms away, several miles away, and some — for the imaginative listener — somewhere out in space. Do you agree with Stockhausen that the traditional idea of tonal and temporal elements is limited?

7. Modern jazz styles require rather keen listening skills for perceptive understanding. What changes in melody have caused this? In rhythm? In form? In improvisation? In artistic function?

8. Why do we experience difficulty in perceiving relationships among musical materials when they occur in inversion or in "crab" style? What is the composer's purpose in utilizing such techniques? Is the composition better as a result?

On Musical Expression

1. Is music in the minor mode always sad? Find examples which disprove this notion.

2. How does music attempt to express ideas of love, hate, anger, death, fear, happiness? Are these expressed the same way in Eastern music?

3. Examine examples of "word painting" in Renaissance and Baroque music. Why was this practice desirable?

4. Listen to the inventions of J. S. Bach. What conclusions can we reach about their expressiveness? Do the same with twelve-tone music. Does this music suggest or refer to any particular sensuous or associative idea? Why would it not be correct to state that it lacks expression?

5. What happens to our emotional responses to music when illustrative titles or program notes are provided? Why do many listeners desire the "story" of the music? In what ways does music express ideas other than by "story-telling?"

6. How are our emotional responses affected when the flow of music reaches a cadential point? Describe the differences in feelings when we hear half cadences, full cadences, and deceptive cadences.

7. Note the changes of expressive character in music when a given melody is treated by harmonic, rhythmic, or other stylistic change. Experiment in class and listen to examples from the literature.

8. Explore the significance of repetition and contrast in musical composition. In what ways are the principles of repetition and contrast generally significant in life?

9. Musical expression has been described in terms of tension and release (struggle-fulfillment, problem-solution, or dissonance-resolution). Are these also characteristic of "practical" experiences? How does the composer deliberately create tensions and releases? Why does he? Are all tensions and releases identical? What causes some musical tension to feel less harsh than others? Under what musical conditions would tension in one context become release in another?

On Comparative Styles

1. Compare the art song with the folk song in matters of text, notation, form, artistic purpose, expression of ideas, and performance practices.

2. Compare Machaut's *Messe de Notre Dame,* Schubert's *Mass in G,* and a contemporary jazz mass. What changes have occurred in musical style? In the service of the mass? Why are there such strong feelings about the mixture of jazz and religion?

3. Listen to examples of music from Oriental cultures. Why does this music sound strange to our ears? How are the rhythms different? Melodies? Textures? Instruments? Harmonies? Performance practices? How could we develop a liking for such music? Consider the notion that "music is a universal language."

4. Compare the timbre and general sonority of organ and orchestral renditions of Bach's *Toccata and Fugue in D Minor.* Compare also two different organ performances. What musical differences are notable in both cases? In the second comparison was the use of another organ of any significance? What instrument did Bach have in mind? What did it sound like? Do we detract or add to the effectiveness of the original music by taking certain liberties in modern performance? Is authenticity in performance a valid goal?

5. Compare musical attitudes towards new music at the turn of the fourteenth, seventeenth, and twentieth centuries.

6. Considering the potential of music to express specific ideas, emotions, or sentiments, compare two examples (appropriately titled): one vocal, the other instrumental. Which lends itself to vivid associations? If we removed the text from the former and tried to add a text to the latter what would happen? Is it valid to learn symphonic themes by associating them with words?

7. Compare the eighteenth-century overture, suite, or symphony with nineteenth-century counterparts. Discover how principles of form remain rather constant while principles of scheme change from era to era.

8. Compare the popular torch song ("I Love You" type) with Grieg's *Ich Liebe Dich* and Wagner's *Tristan und Isolde* on the bases of form, literary value, subtlety of melody and harmony, performance practices, abstractness of meaning, etc.

On Form and Creativity

1. Remove the rhythm from the tune "America" so that the melody remains. Sing and play these tones freely without regard to any particular rhythm. What happens when we add the origi-

nal rhythm? In what way does the rhythmic element function in music like a skeleton does to a body? What would happen if we sang the tune "America" with different rhythms?

2. Utilizing three tones (DO-RE-MI), sing or play (piano, xylophone, tuned water-glasses, etc.) original, freely-created tunes. Explore the broad variety of possibilities. These should be short but exhaustive. Develop concepts of musical repetition and contrast, of simplicity and complexity, of motion by step and by leap, of tendency tones, of rhythmic clarity, of antecedent-consequent phrasing. Extend to five tones, to six, etc. For what reasons would many composers strive to limit the field of musical possibilities in a particular work? Why is it a mark of good composition to utilize successfully an "economy of means?"

3. Explore the science of sound. Which sounds discovered in the classroom environment are purely percussive? Which will emit pitch? (By gently moving an empty chair across the floor, try to obtain harmonics in octaves, fifths, fourths, and with some luck, thirds.) How can we combine these discovered sounds with normal rhythm instruments so that they become musically interesting? Is the melodic factor absolutely necessary? Listen to examples of percussive music by Varèse, Antheil, and others.

What is meant by "playing in tune?" Why do musicians "warm-up?" How is it possible for the bugler to play tunes without the use of valves? What does the inside of the piano look like? What is meant by sympathetic vibration, overtones, pure and tempered tuning? Use the piano tuner as a resource person.

4. Compose original melodies (with and without words) based on scales other than major or minor. Compare, for example, the 7-8 and 4-3 tendencies in Ionian and Dorian modes: the freedom of possibilities with pentatonic and whole-tone scales. Can we create original scales? How does a knowledge of scales help us to understand music? Why was it that some of the earlier modes were discarded in favor of the major and minor? Can we really learn to distinguish tones smaller than the half step? Try creating simple tunes on a stretched string to practice identification of quarter tones or smaller units. (Nettl suggests using a Kunst monochord.)

5. What happens to a single melodic line when it is "harmonized?" Does the addition of another part enrich a melody? Listen to examples of parallel and free organum. Discuss the medieval iedas of perfect intervals as well as concepts of dissonance and consonance. Find the organum in Debussy's En-

gulfed *Cathedral*. (Listen also to Caamano's *Magnificat*, Opus 20 — Louisville Philharmonic, Contemporary Series.)

Harmonize known songs with the Autoharp. What are the limitations? How do these limitations detract from musical interest? Try a variety of Autoharp harmonies to the same melody.

Listen to the harmonic changes in examples of rock 'n' roll. Criticize on the basis of harmonic content. Why would the mature musician consider this kind of music trite? What is meant by a musical cliché?

Listen to and examine Bartók's *Mikrokosmos*. (Some children will be able to play the easier two-part pieces in Volumes I and II. Various instrumental combinations in bass and treble clefs are also possible.) Sing some of the songs with Bartók's accompaniment. Try to improvise his melodies with Autoharp accompaniment. What makes Bartók's music so different? Does this sound like music for study? The teacher should play some of the folk melodies from Grieg's *Album for the Young* with improvised I-IV-V harmonies, and then with the composer's harmonic setting. Compare with Schumann's *Scenes from Childhood* and Stravinsky's *Cinq Doigts*. What is the purpose of the latter? Listen to examples of quartal harmonies, added note chords, and tone clusters. Compare these with traditional tertian harmonies in terms of innovations and tensions, then discuss the relative affects.

6. How does the composer organize extended works so that the listener can become aware of his intent? Analyze binary and ternary forms in school books and apply conceptual understandings to instrumental excerpts. (See the RCA educational recordings.) How are popular songs "organized?" What is the difference between the formal structure and the expressive meaning of "blues" in jazz?

Listen to the first movement of a standard symphony. How does the organization point up both repetition and contrast? How does the over-all ternary form relate to the idea of duality-plurality-unity? Can we find analogous meanings of exposition-development-recapitulation in "practical" experiences? In the organization of a speech? In the writing of a term-paper? In the principles of good salesmanship? In the over-all manner in which we organize our life's activities?

Consider how important the tonic-dominant principle permeated musical form from the eighteenth through the nineteenth centuries. Why does the contemporary composer avoid this principle? Why is literal repetition generally a thing of the past?

What does the contemporary composer expect of his listener? What does the listener expect of the composer?

Composers have written music for performance by school children. Stage a presentation of Hindemith's *Let us Build a City.* Try to utilize various instrumental possibilities and student musicians. (Sixth grade students should not find this work too difficult.) What makes this composition worthwhile for performance by elementary students? How has Hindemith appealed to the interests and abilities of young people?

7. By means of a collective class effort, write an original musical work utilizing song materials, class and/or actual instruments and student performers. Explore the possibilities of involving the school chorus and orchestra as well as other musical resources in the educational and general community. In what ways would an original musical creation by students be more valuable and meaningful than prepared materials found in series books or in other published form? What would students gain in aesthetic and musical understanding by actually assuming the role of the composer?

8. In upper grades, experiment with tape-recorders and basic electronic equipment to explore some of the techniques of tapesichord composition. Discover also through involvement how the twelve chromatic tones can be deliberately formulated into logical tone rows, manipulated into four basic forms and forty-eight possibilities, and finally applied to the actual composition of music. Why did Schoenberg object to the term atonality as a description of his music? What were the consequences of his experiments? Listen to experimental music where not only the melodic material but also other elements are "ordered" (Stockhausen's *Zeitmasse,* Boulez's *Le Marteau sans Maître).* Try composing short pieces as solos or duets according to Schoenberg's system and style and have these played by students. Does this type of composition require an understanding of traditional systems? On what bases? Why did Schoenberg and others feel an artistic need to follow this line of composition?

9. Consider the form of theme and variations. Utilizing a short simple theme, experiment with the number of ways in which variations can occur. Listen to representative recordings. Why are some examples of this form more difficult to perceive than others? What is required of the listener? Why is the variation idea considered to be the heart of "pure" or "serious" jazz?

Formulate a list of examples from the literature that utilize theme and variations as a principle of design. Group them in order of simple to complex. What criteria will be used? Can value concepts be derived on the bases of complexity, abstractness, and subtlety? If one cannot perceive the variations in the second movement of Haydn's *Symphony No. 94 in G Major,* is it probable that Brahms' *Variations on a Theme by Haydn* will be understood? What musical and perceptive skills are necessary for an intelligent understanding of variations? Compare with the passacaglia.

On Socio-cultural Problems

1. How does the contemporary composer earn his living? Why does he often find it difficult to get his works performed and published?

2. Study the composer Charles Ives. For what reasons is he considered an American composer? What is American music? Should it be developed? Discuss the desirable social and political conditions in which musical creativity could thrive. What would happen if a philosophy of art similar to socialist realism were adopted in this country?

3. Discuss the marketing process of a "hit" record. How are profits divided? What is the function of the song plugger? Why does popular music tend to remain popular for a relatively brief period?

4. Music has always been important to religion. Why would certain sects object to instrumental music for worship? What is meant by sacred music? Some religious sects object to the singing of certain music. Are these objections to the actual music (melody rhythm, etc.) or to the text? If secular words were substituted in Schubert's *Ave Maria,* for example, would this lessen its purely musical value? Might it then be considered secular? Think of the meaning of the original text, then analyze the way in which the melody hovers around the tonal center. Is it possible to separate subjective from objective factors by such analysis? Consider and listen to the mixture of sacred and secular ideas in early polytextual motets and parody masses.

Study the reasons for and the results of the Council of Trent. Compare with the musical innovations nurtured by the recent ecumenical movement. Invite speakers from different religious groups (orthodox to reformed) to discuss aesthetic and theological problems which involve music.

5. Consider the probable reasons why various musical instruments were developed and improved. Why is the saxophone not included in the standard symphony orchestra? Are tape re-

corders and frequency modulators "valid" musical instruments? What of the new percussive ideas — sirens, electric bells, airplane motors, brake drums?

Why are there not instructional classes for piano in many public schools just as there are for band and orchestral instruments? Should not the student be given the opportunity to study the guitar and the accordion in public school?

All these ideas serve to illustrate means and ends and to suggest some practical approaches to activate the theoretical foundations. Adaptation and actual implementation to particular levels of instruction will require in the final analysis, not "ivory-tower" speculation, but careful and practical planning by the public school teacher.

It has been the purpose of this book to suggest in a critical manner that music education has reached a point of maturation where the educational challenges of aesthetics must provide for new and important goals. But the need for further research still remains. The problems of musicality (capacity and ability), the aesthetic musical experience, extra-musical and symbolic meanings, intrinsic manifestations of value, criteria for criticism, and the educational functions of all these still reside in the province of theoretical and speculative inquiry. Research in the areas which follow would be of substantial value to the implementation of the proposed ideas for change.

Some Needs for Further Study

1. Project and team research to determine for music, for education, and for society the validity of music education for aesthetic values.

The acceptance and success of aesthetic music education as a necessary branch of education and as a required study for all students at all levels depend, to some extent, on how important this need is felt by music educators and how convincing educators are in influencing others. While individual thinking and speculation with ideas are in keeping with the highest democratic ideals, group endeavors are often more effective in translating ideas into practice. Such research should also serve to clarify further both the need for an articulated program of general music, as well as the kind of teacher preparation necessary to realize aesthetic means and ends.

2. Detailed logical and pedagogical application of alternate value theories to other speculative proposals for music education.

The approach as suggested in this book must withstand open criticism in order to achieve a desirable consensus. Therefore, further theoretical and practical examination of alternate positions is invited. Research should include both curricular suggestions and pedagogical approaches.

3. Definition and clarification of what is expressly implied by the "musically educated."

Such studies would search for norms in aesthetic and musical behavior among various social types. Methods of research could include case studies, questionnaires, personal interviews, and psychological testing, culminating in more precise definitions of maturation in the process of musical growth.

4. Further clarification and experimentation in the psychological nature of music and the affective nature of man, supplementing — by verification or negation — the findings of Seashore, Meyer, Mursell, Langer, and others.

The needs for further experimental research in the psychology of music education are still obvious. The lack of substantial agreement concerning the nature and measurement of musicality does not help to prevent educational confusion. A program of aesthetic music education must be based on sound psychological principles which point up a valid relation of music to the human senses and intellect. Extensive studies of what reactions to music are singularly musical, and of the paradoxes in musical meanings would do much to clarify the aesthetic experience for education. Controlled classroom studies in campus laboratory schools would probably offer the most effective experimental beginnings.

5. Studies to determine aesthetic means and ends wherein contemporary music can assume a more significant role in education.

The problems of modern music must become the concern of the educator. Aside from more thoroughgoing programs of musical preparation, the resolution of these problems depends upon the application of aesthetic criteria in areas of new and controversial music. Studies should also show how more contemporary materials can be introduced in music series books not only for listening purposes but for singing, playing, and creative writing. (Similar studies for pre-Baroque music would also be applicable.)

6. Studies to determine effective ways by which music educators can assume a more active role in the variety and quality of music transmitted by mass media.

Research in this area should result in frank appraisals of the economic controls which bear on the aesthetic functions of music education. The conditioning of mass musical values through radio and television programming is highly effective. Such influence cannot be considered as separate from the educational jurisdiction. Avenues for mutual interests and goals, through arbitrary understandings, must be established for the purposes of aesthetic refinement and educational effectiveness.

7. Research that would indicate how the aesthetic discipline serves to color and enrich the intellectual and scientific.

The use of music as an aesthetic embellishment to other areas of study entails concentrated study of the question of intrinsic and extrinsic musical values. Significant conclusions should aid substantially in the establishment of rational concepts.

8. Analyses of the criticisms directed against contemporary music education by musicians, educators, and laymen to determine the degree of emphasis attributed by these groups to the aesthetic functions of music.

Such studies would point up mutual understandings for constructive purposes. Aesthetic means and ends gain strength by accepting and translating valid criticisms.

9. Socio-cultural research to clarify the desirable role of music education in improving tastes and standards; in emphasizing logical methods of musical inquiry; and in presupposing universality and world outlook.

How can the theoretical level of aesthetic discrimination be transformed into a working reality through education? Is it really possible to fashion measures for musical value which would be universally acceptable? Are there musically aesthetic needs common to different cultures? Are there common, desirable educational yardsticks that would meet a consensus of opinion among members of the International Society for Music Education?

10. Determination of the types of studies in philosophy, aesthetics, sociology, and anthropology that would be most beneficial to potential music educators, performers, composers, and musicologists.

Conducted on multi-disciplined levels of inquiry, results of research in this area would indicate the means by which preparatory studies in general culture serve to broaden perspectives in artistic and educational fields. Core learning and team-teaching procedures are also worthy of further investigation.

11. Studies to indicate the kind and degree of influence of public school music on the musical values of the community.

Such research should not only report statistically on the state of musical affairs in the community, but also compare and correlate statistical information with the aesthetic objectives of formal education. Does the school function to enhance musical behavior? In what ways can an improved rapport beyond high school or college be nurtured? How can discriminatory levels of appreciation be rationalized to serve the unique needs of various social and ethnic groups? (Similar research on state and national levels would also be beneficial.)

12. Definition and elaboration of the aesthetic values of music in relation to general social functions, i.e., criminal rehabilitation, therapeutic needs, industry, leisure, etc.

The validity of the musical arts for both aesthetic and non-aesthetic social purposes requires further substantiation. For example, is it really the music or the experience of music-making (or pleasurable diversion) that is therapeutic? Are there non-musical activities that could substitute just as well for the purely musical? When music functions in these utilitarian ways, what of aesthetic values?

13. Further studies in comparative music and music education that would reveal how other cultures validate the aesthetic function.

Educational studies in this area have been concerned mostly with comparative methods and curricula. Beginnings in the establishment of an international rapport in music and music education have been so encouraging, that research in intra-cultural aesthetics is already under way. Recent contributions in ethnomusicology indicate an increasing interest in non-Western music. The possibilities here for appropriate studies in music education are inviting.

These recommendations for further study, are not mutually exclusive. Each serves to enhance and to stimulate the other. In this manner, a body of knowledge can be accumulated for the purpose of applying derived understandings to concerted action in the search for aesthetic improvement through music education.

BIBLIOGRAPHY

A. Books

Adams, George P., and William P. Montague (eds.). *Contemporary American Philosophy.* New York: The MacMillan Co., 1930.

Adamson, John E. *The Theory of Education in Plato's Republic.* New York: The MacMillan Co., 1903.

Allen, Warren D. *Philosophies of Music History.* New York: American Book Co., 1939.

Apel, Willi. *Harvard Dictionary of Music.* Cambridge: Harvard University Press, 1956.

Bacon, Ernst. *Words on Music.* Syracuse: Syracuse University Press, 1960.

Barzun, Jacques. *Music in American Life.* New York: Doubleday and Co., Inc., 1958.

Beardsley, Monroe C. *Aesthetics: Problems in the Philosophy of Criticism.* New York: Harcourt, Brace and Co., 1958.

Birge, Edward B. *History of Public School Music in the United States.* Washington, D. C.: Music Educators National Conference, 1966.

Brameld, Theodore. *Education for the Emerging Age.* New York: Harper and Bros., 1961.

———. *Philosophies of Education in Cultural Perspective.* New York: Dryden Press, 1955.

———. *Toward a Reconstructed Philosophy of Education.* New York: Dryden Press, 1956.

Broudy, Harry S. *Building a Philosophy of Education,* second edition. Englewood Cliffs, New Jersey: Prentice-Hall, Inc., 1961.

Brubacher, John S. *Modern Philosophies of Education.* New York: McGraw-Hill Book Co., Inc., 1950.

Chambers, Frank P. *The History of Taste.* New York: Columbia University Press, 1932.

Counts, George S. *The Challenge of Soviet Education.* New York: McGraw-Hill Book Co., 1957.

Davison, Archibald. *Music Education in America.* New York: Harper and Bros., 1926.

Dewey, John. *Art as Experience.* New York: Putnam's & Coward-McCann, 1959.

———. *Democracy and Education.* New York: The MacMillan Co., 1922.

———. *Reconstruction in Philosophy.* Boston: Beacon Press, 1957.

———. *School and Society.* Chicago: University of Chicago Press, 1915.

Dorian, Frederick. *Commitment to Culture: Art Patronage in Europe, Its Significance for America.* Pittsburgh: University of Pittsburgh Press, 1964.

Eby, Frederick and Charles F. Arrowood. *The History and Philosophy of Education, Ancient and Medieval.* Englewood Cliffs, New Jersey: Prentice-Hall, Inc., 1940.

Fleming, William. *Art and Ideas.* New York: Holt, Rinehart and Winston, 1963.

Galbraith, John K. *The Affluent Society.* Boston: Houghton Mifflin Co., 1958.

Grout, Donald J. *A History of Western Music.* New York: W. W. Norton and Co., 1960.

Hanslick, E. *The Beautiful in Music,* translated by J. Cohen. New York: Liberal Arts Press, 1957.

Hauser, Arnold. *The Philosophy of Art History.* New York: Alfred A. Knopf, 1959.

———. *The Social History of Art,* Vols. I and II. New York: Alfred A. Knopf, 1951.

Hechinger, Fred M. *The Big Red Schoolhouse.* New York: Doubleday and Co., 1959.

Helmholtz, H. L. *On the Sensations of Tone.* New York: Dover Publications, 1954.

Heyl, Bernard C. *New Bearings in Esthetics and Art Criticism.* New Haven: Yale University Press, 1943.

Hiller, Lejaren A., and Leonard M. Isaacson. *Experimental Music.* New York: McGraw-Hill Book Co., 1959.

Hindemith, Paul. *Craft of Musical Composition,* translated by A. Mendel, Book I. New York: Associated Music Publishers, Inc., 1942.

———. *The Composer's World.* Cambridge: Harvard University Press, 1952.

Hollingshead, August B. *Elmtown's Youth.* New York: John Wiley and Sons, Inc., 1949.

Jowett, Benjamin. *The Basic Works of Aristotle,* Book VIII, Chapter VII. New York: Random House, 1941.

Juilliard School of Music. *The Juilliard Report on Teaching the Literature and Materials of Music.* New York: W. W. Norton and Co., 1953.

Kandel, I. L. *The New Era in Education.* New York: Houghton Mifflin Co., 1955.

Kant, Immanuel. *Critique of Judgment,* translated by J. H. Bernard. London: MacMillan and Co., 1951.

Kline, George L. (ed.). *Soviet Education.* New York: Columbia University Press, 1957.

Krone (Perham), Mrs. Beatrice. *Music in the New School.* Chicago: Neil A. Kjos Music Co., 1941.

Langer, Suzanne K. *Feeling and Form.* New York: Philosophical Library Inc., 1953.

———. *Philosophy in a New Key.* Cambridge: Harvard University Press, 1957.

———. (ed.). *Reflections on Art.* Baltimore: Johns Hopkins Press, 1958.

Leichtentritt, Hugo. *Musical Form.* Cambridge: Harvard University Press, 1951.

Leonhard, Charles and Robert W. House. *Foundations and Principles of Music Education.* New York: McGraw-Hill Book Co., 1959.

Lowenthal, Leo. *Literature, Popular Culture and Society.* Englewood Cliffs, New Jersey: Prentice-Hall, Inc., 1960.

Lundin, Robert. *An Objective Psychology of Music.* New York: The Ronald Press Co., 1953.

Maritain, Jacques. *The Responsibility of the Artist.* New York: Charles Scribner's Sons, 1960.

Mason, Lowell. *Manual of the Boston Academy of Music,* Seventh Edition. Boston: 1851.

Mayne, Thomas R. *Music in the Modern School.* Philadelphia: David McKay Co., 1934.

Meyer, Leonard B. *Emotion and Meaning in Music.* Chicago: University of Chicago Press, 1956.

Moles, Abraham. *Information Theory and Esthetic Perception,* translated by Joel E. Cohen. Urbana: University of Illinois Press, 1965.

Morris, Van Cleve. *Philosophy and the American School.* Boston: Houghton Mifflin Co., 1961.

Mueller, John. *The American Symphony Orchestra.* Bloomington: Indiana University Press, 1951.

Mumford, Lewis. *Art and Technics.* New York: Columbia University Press, 1952.

Mursell, James L. *Education for Musical Growth.* New York: Ginn and Co., 1948.

——. *Human Values in Music Education.* New York: Silver Burdett Co., 1934.

——. *Music and the Classroom Teacher.* New York: Silver Burdett Co., 1951.

——. *Music Education: Principles and Programs.* New York: Silver Burdett Co., 1956.

—— and Mabelle Glenn. *The Psychology of School Music Teaching.* New York: Silver Burdett Co., 1931.

Nettl, Bruno. *Theory and Method in Ethnomusicology.* New York: Free Press, 1964.

Ortega y Gasset, Jose. *The Dehumanization of Art.* New York: Doubleday and Co., Inc., 1956.

Ostransky, Leroy (ed.). *Perspectives on Music.* Englewood Cliffs, New Jersey: Prentice-Hall, Inc., 1963.

Parker, De Witt. *The Principles of Aesthetics.* New York: F. S. Crofts and Co., 1946.

Pitts, Lilla Bella. *The Music Curriculum in a Changing World.* New York: Silver Burdett Co., 1944.

Plato. *The Republic,* translated by B. Jowett. New York: Clarendon Press, 1881.

Portnoy, Julius. *Music in the Life of Man.* New York: Holt, Rinehart and Winston, 1963.

——. *The Philosopher and Music.* New York: The Humanities Press, 1955.

Prall, D. W. *Aesthetic Analysis*. New York: Thomas Y. Crowell Co., 1936.

Rabinovitch, Israel. *Of Jewish Music: Ancient and Modern*. Montreal: The Book Center, 1952.

Rader, Melvin (ed.). *A Modern Book of Esthetics*. New York: Henry Holt and Co., 1952.

Riesman, David (et al.). *The Lonely Crowd: A Study of Changing American Character*. New Haven: Yale University Press, 1950.

Rugg, Harold and William Withers. *Social Foundations of Education*. Englewood Cliffs, New Jersey: Prentice-Hall, Inc., 1955.

Russell, Bertrand. *The Problems of Philosophy*. New York: Oxford University Press, 1959.

Santayana, George. *The Sense of Beauty*. New York: Modern Library, 1955.

Schiller, Friedrich. *On the Aesthetic Education of Man*, translated by R. Snell. London: Routledge and Kegan Paul Ltd., 1954.

Schoenberg, Arnold. *Style and Idea*. New York: Philosophical Library Inc., 1950.

Sorokin, Pitrim A. *Social and Cultural Dynamics*. New York: American Book Co., 1937.

Stolnitz, Jerome. *Aesthetics and Philosophy of Art Criticism: A Critical Introduction*. Boston: Houghton Mifflin Co., 1960.

Stravinsky, Igor. *The Poetics of Music*, translated by A. Knodel and I. Dahl. New York: Random House, 1947.

Thomson, Virgil. *The State of Music*. New York: William Morrow and Co., 1939.

Tolstoy, Leo. *What is Art?*, translated by A. Maude. New York: Oxford University Press, 1962.

Walford, Edward. *The Politics and Economics of Aristotle*. London: George Bell and Sons, 1908.

Weitz, Morris. *Problems in Aesthetics*. New York: The MacMillan Co., 1959.

B. Publications of the Government, Learned Societies, and Other Organizations

Committee on Rural Music. "Standard Course for the Music Training of the Grade Teacher," *Journal of Proceedings*. Chicago: Music Supervisors' National Conference, 1925.

Ernst, Karl D. and Charles L. Gary. *Music in General Education*. Washington, D. C.: Music Educators National Conference, 1965.

Kaplan, Max (chairman). *Music in a Changing World*. Report for Music in American Life Commission VIII. Washington: Music Educators National Conference, 1958.

Kendel, John. "Music as an Exponent of the Democratic Process," *Music Education Conference Review*. Austin, Texas: The University of Texas, College of Fine Arts, August, 1945.

Henry, Nelson B. (ed.). *Basic Concepts in Music Education,* Fifty-seventh Yearbook of the National Society for the Study of Education, Part I. Chicago: Distributed by the University of Chicago Press, 1958.

Lawler, Vanett (ed.). "The Function of Music in the Secondary-School Curriculum," *Bulletin of the National Association of Secondary School Principals,* 36-8, November, 1952.

Leonhard, Charles. "The Next Ten Years in Music Education," *Council for Research in Music Education,* Bulletin No. 7. Urbana: University of Illinois, Spring, 1966.

McEachern, Edna. "Musical Training for Grade Teachers," *Yearbook of the Music Supervisors' National Conference.* Chicago: Music Supervisors' National Conference, 1927.

Morgan, Hazel N. (ed.). *Music in American Education.* Chicago: Music Educators National Conference, 1955.

Music Education Research Council. *Musical Development of the Classroom Teacher,* Bulletin No. 5. Chicago: Music Educators National Conference, 1951.

NEA Research Bulletin. "Music in the Public Schools," Volume 41, No. 2. Washington: Research Division, National Education Association, May, 1963, 56-59.

Planning Committee, Secondary School Division, Eastern Division. *Music in Secondary Education.* Boston: Music Educators National Conference, February, 1955.

Rockefeller Panel Report on the Future of Theatre, Dance, Music in America. *The Performing Arts—Problems and Prospects.* New York: McGraw-Hill Book Co., 1965.

Santa Cruz, Domingo. "Music and International Understanding," *Music in Education.* Report on the International Conference on the Role and Place of Music in the Education of Youth and Adults, Brussels, 1953. New York: Columbia University Press, 1955.

United States Office of Education, *Education in the U.S.S.R.* (Bul. 1957, No. 14). Washington, D. C.: Government Printing Office, 1957.

Yale Seminar on Music Education. *Music in Our Schools: A Search for Improvement.* Washington, D. C.: U.S. Department of Health, Education and Welfare, 1964.

C. Periodicals

Albertson, Marjorie. "We Not Only Teach Music—We Also Teach Children," *Music Educators Journal,* 46:99-103, February-March, 1960.

Austin, Virginia D. "Music Can Reach All Children," *Music Journal,* 22:26, May, 1954.

Baird, Forrest J. "Music as an Aid to Recreation," *Music Journal,* 16:26, 69, January, 1958.

———. "Music in a Changing Curriculum," *Music Journal,* 17:70, March, 1959.

Bauman, D. E. "A Society for Lovers of Symphonic Music," *Soviet Education*, 3:50, January, 1960.

Beattie, John W. "Musical Education in 1975," *Educational Music Magazine*, 35:10-12, January, 1956.

Bernat, Robert. "Do We Really Have a Commitment to Culture?" *Carnegie Review*, No. 4, Spring, 1965, 3-12.

Blowers, Hilda. "Philosophy of Music Education," *Music Journal*, 15:42, January, 1957.

Broudy, Harry S. "Does Music Education Need a Philosophy?" *Music Educators Journal*, 44:28-29, November-December, 1957.

Burnsworth, Charles C. "The Self-Contained Classroom Reconsidered," *Music Educators Journal*, 48:41, November-December, 1961.

Chauncey, Beatrice. "Elementary Music Teaching," *Music Journal*, 16:46, February, 1958.

Clayman, Charles S. "Value and the Teacher," *Journal of Education*, Boston University, School of Education, 143:23-27, April, 1961.

Coolidge, Arlan. "A Look at Music Education and America's Juke Box Culture," *Music Educators Journal*, 42:37, February-March, 1956.

Dennis, Charles M. "Music's Message for the Millions," *Phi Delta Kappan*, 35:300-302, May, 1954.

Dewey, John. "Meaning of Value," *Journal of Philosophy*, February, 1925, 131.

Eads, Joseph W. "Employees Want Music," *Music Journal*, 2:11, November, 1953.

Elkan, Ida. "Music Vs. Delinquency," *Music Journal*, 16:61, September, 1958.

Ernst, Karl D. "Where Do We Go From Here?" *Music Educators Journal*, 40:17, January, 1954.

Fowler, Charles B. "Discovery Method: Its Relevance for Music Education," *Journal of Research in Music Education*, XIV, Summer, 1966, 126.

Haines, Aubrey B. "Music in Industry," *Music Journal*, 17:30, February, 1959.

Hallman, Ralph J. "Aesthetic Motivation in the Creative Arts," *Journal of Aesthetics and Art Criticism*, Vol. 23, No. 4, Summer, 1965, 453-459.

Harrell, Jean G. "Issues in Music Aesthetics," *Journal of Aesthetics and Art Criticism*, Vol. 23, No. 2, Winter, 1964, 197-206.

Hartshorn, William C. "Integrity in Music Education," *Music Educators Journal*, 46:29, September-October, 1959.

————. "Music in General Education," *Music Educators Journal*, 42:26, September-October, 1955.

Horn, Francis H. "Music for Everyone," *Music Educators Journal*, 42:27, February-March, 1956.

Howie, Marguerite R. "Karl Mannheim and the Sociology of Knowledge," *Journal of Education*, Boston University, School of Education, 143:55-71, April, 1961.

Hume, Paul. "Report on American Music," *Music Journal,* 17:12-13, October, 1959.

Jarvis, Ellis A. "The Fine Arts in the Age of Automation," *Music Educators Journal,* 45:19-21, January, 1959.

Kaplan, Max. "Music, Community and Social Change," *Music Educators Journal,* 43:64-67, September-October, 1956.

Koontz, James E. "Music and General Education," *Music Educators Journal,* 42:20, January, 1956.

Krash, Otto. "Is Music Educational?", *Music Educators Journal,* 43:64, February-March, 1957.

Krone, Max T. "Jazz and the General Music Class," *Music Educators Journal,* 45:23, June-July, 1959.

Landeck, Beatrice. "Standards of Literature and Performance at the Primary Level," *Music Educators Journal,* 43:54, November-December, 1956.

Leonhard, Charles. "Research: Philosophy and Esthetics," *Journal of Research in Music Education,* III, Spring, 1955, 23-26.

Lindsay, Howard. "Governmental Recognition of Music," *Music Journal,* 18:28, 94, March, 1960.

Lissa, Zofia. "Aesthetic Functions of Silence and Rests in Music," *Journal of Aesthetics and Art Criticism,* Vol. 22, No. 4, Summer, 1964, 443-454.

Madison, Thurber H. "An Adventure in Concepts," *Music Educators Journal,* 44:28, January, 1958.

Mannheim, R. L., and Alice Cummins. "Musical Traits of Racial Groups," *Sociology and Social Research,* 45:56-65, October, 1960.

Mayfield, Alpha C. "Music and Recreation," *Music Journal,* 13:31-33, February, 1955.

McKay, George F. "Toward Cultural Definition," *Journal of Research in Music Education,* III, Fall, 1955, 92-100.

McLellan, Beth. "Music Training for Elementary Teachers," *Music Educators Journal,* 35:19, April, 1949.

Meyer, Leonard B. "Some Remarks on Value and Greatness in Music," *Journal of Aesthetics and Art Criticism,* Vol. 17, June, 1959.

Miller, Rosemary. "Music for Everyone?", *Music Journal,* 16:42, January, 1958.

Molnar, John W. "Changing Aspects of American Culture as Reflected in the MENC," *Journal of Research in Music Education,* VII, Fall, 1959, 174.

Mones, Leon. "Music and Education in Our American Democracy," *Music Educators Journal,* 45:27-30, September-October, 1958.

Munro, Paul. "Aesthetics of Science: Its Development in America," *Journal of Aesthetics and Art Criticism,* Vol. 19, 1961, 161.

Munro, Thomas. "Recent Developments in Aesthetics in America," *Journal of Aesthetics and Art Criticism,* Vol. 23, No. 2, Winter, 1964, 251-260.

Nettl, Paul. "Politics and Music," *Music Journal*, 16:14, 57-58, October, 1958.

Nye, Robert E. "Some Thoughts and Theories about Secondary School Music," *Music Educators Journal*, 45-26, November-December, 1958.

Phelps, Roger P. "Research in Music and Music Education," *Music Educators Journal*, 46:51-52, June-July, 1960.

Rosen, Charles. "The Proper Study of Music," *Perspectives of New Music*, Fall, 1962, 80-88.

Schiller, Jerome. "An Alternative to Aesthetic Disinterestedness," *Journal of Aesthetics and Art Criticism*, Vol. 22, No. 3, 1964, 295-302.

Schoen, Max. "Psychological Problems in Musical Art," *Journal of Research in Music Education*, III, Spring, 1955, 27-39.

Schwadron, Abraham A. "Aesthetic Values in Music Education," *Music Journal*, May, 1964, 42.

———. "Contemporary Chamber Music for the Clarinet," *The Instrumentalist*, Vol. 9, No. 11, June, 1965, 73-76.

———. "Musical Aesthetics: A Review and Critique," *Music Educators Journal*, 51:69-71, 181-183, February-March, 1965.

———. "In Defense of the Special Music Teacher," *Music Educators Journal*, 52:62-64, September-October, 1965.

———. "Music and the Classroom Teacher," *Music Journal*, 24:64,78, February, 1966.

Sparling, Edward J. "Music for the Masses," *Music Educators Journal*, 43:28,30, November-December, 1956.

Steiner, George. "The Imaginary Concert Hall," *The Reporter*, 22:40, January, 1960.

Sunderman, Lloyd F. "Great Issues in Music Education," *Education*, 74:3-10, September, 1953.

Thompson, Frank. "Government Support of Music," *Music Journal*, 1957 Annual, 76.

Tischler, Hans. "The Aesthetic Experience," *The Music Review*, 17:189, 1956.

Travelstead, Chester C. "Basic Objectives of Music Education at the Secondary Level, *Music Educators Journal*, 44:24-26, January, 1958.

Waldrop, Evelyn B. "Education or Entertainment," *Music Journal*, 14:16, December, 1954.

Wegener, Frank C. "The Aesthetic Function of Man," *Educational Music Magazine*, 34:8-9, November, 1954.

Williams, Albert S. "Music and Crime Prevention," *Music Journal*, 15:11, 52, October, 1957.

Williams, Arthur L. "Who May Study Music?", *Music Journal*, 1957 Annual, 74.

Zack, Melvin L. "Basic Piano Skills for the General Music Teacher," *Music Educators Journal*, 46:93, September-October, 1959.

D. Articles in Collections

Baensch, Otto. "Art and Feeling," *Reflections on Art,* Suzanne K. Langer, editor, pp. 10-36.

Broudy, Harry S. "A Realistic Philosophy of Music Education," *Basic Concepts in Music Education,* Nelson B. Henry, editor, pp. 62-87.

Kluckhohn, Clyde. "Values and Value Orientation," *Toward a General Theory of Action,* Parsons and Shils, editors, pp. 388-403.

MacMurray, Foster. "Pragmatism in Music Education," *Basic Concepts in Music Education,* Nelson B. Henry, editor, pp. 30-61.

Madison, Thurber N. "The Need for New Concepts in Music Education," *Basic Concepts in Music Education,* Nelson B. Henry, editor, pp. 3-29.

McKay, George F. "The Range of Musical Experience," *Basic Concepts in Music Education,* Nelson B. Henry, editor, pp. 123-139.

Mueller, John H. "Music and Education: A Sociological Approach," *Basic Concepts in Music Education,* Nelson B. Henry, editor, pp. 88-122.

Reid, Louis A. "Beauty and Significance," *Reflections on Art,* Suzanne K. Langer, editor, pp. 37-61.

Sullivan, J. W. N. "Music as Expression," *Problems in Aesthetics,* M. Weitz, editor, pp. 410-418.

E. Unpublished Materials

Fowler, Charles B. "A Reconstructionist Philosophy of Music Education." Unpublished Doctoral dissertation, Mus.A.D., Boston University, 1964.

Hetenyi, Lazzlo J. "Outline of a Philosophic Position and its Application to an Introductory Music Program in General Education." Unpublished Doctoral dissertation, D.Ed., Michigan State University, 1956.

Hill, Francis. "The Place of Music in Educational Philosophy," Unpublished Master's thesis, M.M.E., Texas Christian University, 1951.

McCorkle, T. S. "Recent American Educational Theories on the Place and Function of the Fine Arts in the Public School Program," Unpublished Doctoral dissertation, D.Ed., University of Texas, 1942.

Parker, Olin G. "A Study of the Relation of Aesthetic Sensitivity to Musical Ability, Intelligence and Socioeconomic Status." Unpublished Doctoral dissertation, D.Ed., University of Kansas, 1961.

Reimer, Bennett. "Common Dimensions of Aesthetic and Religious Experience." Unpublished Doctoral dissertation, D.Ed., Music Education, University of Illinois, 1963.

Schwadron, Abraham A. "An Interpretation of Philosophy and Aesthetics for Contemporary Music Education." Unpublished Doctoral dissertation, Mus.A.D., Boston University, 1962.